MILWAUKEE AVENUE

MILWAUKEE AVENUE

COMMUNITY RENEWAL IN MINNEAPOLIS

ROBERT ROSCOE

THE
H
History
PRESS

Published by The History Press
Charleston, SC 29403
www.historypress.net

All photos courtesy of the author unless otherwise noted.

First published 2014

ISBN 978-1-5402-0994-8

Library of Congress CIP data applied for.

Contents

CONTENTS

CONTENTS

Contents

Published by The History Press
Charleston, SC 29403
www.historypress.net

All photos courtesy of the author unless otherwise noted.

First published 2014

ISBN 978-1-5402-0994-8

Library of Congress CIP data applied for.

MILWAUKEE AVENUE
COMMUNITY RENEWAL IN MINNEAPOLIS

ROBERT ROSCOE

THE
History
PRESS

Acknowledgements

One of the most significant events in my life took place during the years 1972 to 1981, when I became swept into the intense campaign by the Seward West Project Area Committee (PAC) to thwart a public agency's plans to obliterate a traditional nineteenth-century neighborhood in south Minneapolis and later became one of the planners who helped revitalize the thirty-five-block area. Accordingly, I dedicate this book to the Seward West PAC. What we members achieved is immeasurable and has contributed to the neighborhood, the city and architectural preservation. In particular, Tony Scallon's immense intelligence and decisive leadership became a critical force in guiding all of us. Read my words: Seward West and Milwaukee Avenue would not have been rescued without Tony Scallon. The multi-talented Don Barton became an inspiration, helping in all our efforts from start to completion. Also, among the many PAC members to be commended for their prodigious efforts are Kathy Johnson Williams, Steve Swanson, Kent Robbins and Rudi Anders. Jeri Reilly wonderfully contributed to shaping this book's content and structure.

I also wish to thank Minneapolis Housing and Redevelopment Authority (HRA) staff members Bob Scroggins and Tom Goodoien, whose work greatly predicated the success of Seward West.

I really appreciate my wife, Sally, who made both of us stronger during the sometimes trying circumstances and whose pleasing demeanor served the whole of the effort.

ACKNOWLEDGEMENTS

I must thank Greg Donofrio, PhD, assistant professor and director of Heritage Conservation and Preservation at the University of Minnesota School of Architecture, who urged me and inspired me to write this book, as well as his wife and preservation scholar Erin Coryell, who skillfully guided me in various exercises in my early writing.

Also deserving of my gratitude is David Unowsky, whose talents in the publishing world led me to this great publisher, The History Press.

Introduction

Background

In the 1950s, America's economic and social ambitions were no longer taking place in its cities. Disinvestment in central city neighborhoods caused the deterioration of houses in large areas, reducing real estate values and the number of residents. Government urban renewal programs reasoned that clearing away blight with the blades of bulldozers was an effective solution. In the early years of these programs, city agencies faced no significant opposition by the people most affected. By the 1970s, two decades of federal urban renewal programs had promised urban nirvanas but delivered American cities with mostly unsuccessful outcomes, the most tragic being the wholesale obliteration of inner-city neighborhoods.

In the 1970s, a politically savvy and hardworking neighborhood organization, the Seward West Project Area Committee (PAC), outmaneuvered a public agency's renewal plan to demolish approximately 70 percent of a thirty-five-block neighborhood in Minneapolis, Minnesota. Demolition would have included all of the houses on Milwaukee Avenue, a half-hidden and extremely narrow two-block-long street flanked by small brick houses, many with similar gingerbread-style porches.

The similarity of forms on Milwaukee Avenue, coupled with the narrowness of the street and its 1,400-foot length, provide a distinct beginning, middle and end, evoking a sense of intimacy and scale quite different from the surrounding neighborhood. Built in the 1880s, many of

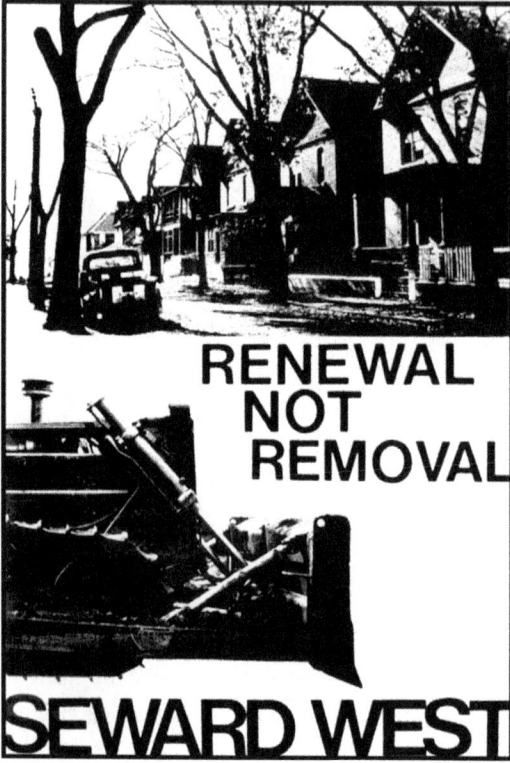

Left: "Renewal Not Removal." This PAC poster intended to create interest in the cause to save the neighborhood.

Below: The last of the Milwaukee Railroad Shops buildings. The shops once covered a large area just three blocks away from the south end of Milwaukee Avenue. Many railroad workers and their families lived on the street.

these structures were the first homes in Minneapolis for immigrant families of Northern European workers who labored in the nearby Milwaukee Railroad yards and industrial shops.

Jeri Reilly and I were staff workers for PAC. Our research led to Milwaukee Avenue's designation as a historic district for its role in immigrant housing and its importance as an unorthodox residential environment. We began the urban design process for the street and created architectural drawings for a pedestrian walkway and related open spaces, perimeter parking areas, restoration of its houses and new compatible infill structures within its four-block area. *Milwaukee Avenue* relates our firsthand experiences during the neighborhood's seven-year struggle. Eventually, PAC's rehabilitation-oriented program preserved the neighborhood's traditional character, having accomplished the basic governmental objectives of creating attractive and affordable housing, with many of the houses rehabilitated by the homeowners themselves.

This book offers a unique presentation of determined citizens who saved their neighborhood in a decade that changed history. It will discuss how historic preservation's role served as an essential portrayal of a microcosm of the history of the 1970s, in which this neighborhood became the locus of fundamental social and political change that still influences how we live and think today. Milwaukee Avenue and the surrounding Seward West neighborhood represent the emergence and accomplishments of citizen participation as an active agent of cultural and political change occurring in America at that time. Its emphasis on rehab rather than demolition influenced a transformative effect on cities, aided by the emerging embrace of historic preservation. Seward West emerged at the beginning of the women's movement and the caring for the stewardship of our environment. The reintroduction of backyard vegetable gardens brought natural foods back to kitchen tables. An alternative local economy in and around Seward West generated the cooperative model that established cooperatively operated grocery stores, cafés, bicycle shops, child-care facilities and community-based health clinics. These enterprises flourish in many of our neighborhoods today. History, once exclusively a curatorial discipline of the accomplishments of the elite and powerful, began to examine the role and cultural contributions of the working class in historical development.

The history of Milwaukee Avenue's planned destruction and triumphant rescue is less than fifty years old at the time of this writing. The retracing of the critical factors that defined its successful outcome came about by my recollected memories and those of contributor Jeri Reilly. Lacking the detached observers' viewpoint, our close-at-hand writing renders portrayals of our work and the actions of our fellow activists, framing the narrative history of the moment and the zeitgeist that changed the neighborhood.

Much of the manuscript is based on our direct experience and observations. Significant portions of the text are accounts from various people involved in the process whom I recently interviewed for comments about their experiences and to jog my own memory (knowing that memory can be a fallible instrument). (A relevant side note: a few of the former PAC members I interviewed were very much on the opposite side during the highly contentious and bitter infighting within PAC, and I wanted to make sure my recorded statements in this book were not biased by what might have been my self-serving beliefs at that time. Interestingly, during these interviews, I noticed that the intervening three decades had lent a partial meeting of minds, while certain longtime attitudes were noticeably kept unspoken.)

Also important were documents copied from city archives; my collection of drawings and meeting minutes from the Minneapolis Planning Commission, Minneapolis Heritage Preservation Commission and the Seward West PAC; and letters contributed by former PAC members. These accounts compile a firsthand history embedded in the spine of this book's pages that make for a unique publication.

"WHAT AN INTERESTING STREET!"

In my mind,
I can't study war no more.
Save the people!
Save the children!
Save the country, now!
—Laura Nyro, "Save the Country," 1969

In the early 1970s, pre-renewal times, passersby looking up close at a Milwaukee Avenue house would see its uneven stucco façade with zigzag cracks and several crevices showing the brick underneath, windows in various states of disrepair, a front porch with a sagging roof, cracked boards and ill-fitting aluminum storm windows and an empty opening where a screen door once stood but had been missing for some time.

However, when looking at many of these houses aligned in wider view, the decrepitude would appear picturesque—an assemblage of textures composed by time-transforming surfaces. At the time, this was what American tourists would travel to Europe to visit, seeking to capture the images on Kodachrome

In this circa 1971 photo, kids are playing kickball on Milwaukee Avenue at its former intersection with East Twenty-second Street.

film. But in America, city planners would classify these conditions as physical degeneracy, and they would seek to capture it in the maws of bulldozers. Peoples' first glimpses could cause reactions varying from, "This place looks very dangerous" to "What an interesting street!"

In 1970, Jeri Reilly noted, "Milwaukee Ave and much of the neighborhood was on death row—with no chance for reprieve." We heard the refrain 'These houses cannot be saved' everywhere we turned. Everyone said it. At first it was hard to argue otherwise. It took us awhile to find the vocabulary. It was the beginning of our romantic education." At the time, the residents of the Seward West neighborhood were mostly older, low-income people who had been left behind or newly arrived young people who were eagerly facing their futures. In an introduction to Cyn Collins's book *West Bank Boogie,* Garrison Keillor wrote about the music scene on the nearby West Bank at this time, a scene that included musicians living on Milwaukee Avenue. Keillor writes, "We were young people trying to scrape up an authentic past. We accepted poverty."

The genesis of the effort to save Milwaukee Avenue began on the nearby University of Minnesota campus. When the news broke that President Richard Nixon had ordered the secret bombing of Cambodia in 1970, a time when people were longing and expecting the war to wind down, the country reacted. A general strike was called at the University of Minnesota. Jeri remembers helicopters flying over Northrup Mall, dropping canisters of mace, and that the students who were not striking were forced to flee their classrooms, tears streaming down their faces.

Typical pre-renewal workman's cottages at 2109, 2111, 2117, 2121 and 2125 Milwaukee Avenue, 1972.

An antiwar organization, Students Against the War, called a meeting of the strikers, who were exhorted to do PR work by going into the neighborhoods and telling people why they were striking. Jeri was part of a small group from Seward West—although the group didn't know it was called that at the time. She recalls, "We divvied up the streets and set a time to report back to the group. At the first door I knocked on at a house on Milwaukee Avenue, the people had only a dim idea of what was going on at the university. Rather indifferent to Vietnam, they had their own war: the urban renewal plan. They'd ask me, 'Do you know what's going on? Do you know when they're going to start tearing down the houses?' Well, that was news to me." When they met up to discuss the antiwar sentiment in the neighborhood, they realized they had seen the close-at-home beginnings of a new cause with its own vocabulary, which included words like "urban renewal plan," "demolition," "relocation" and "HRA."

During that time, my wife, Sally, and I were also attracted to Seward West by the cheap rent, and we found a clean place for our new family located close to the university, where I was attending architecture school. I was born in a small town in northern Minnesota, and when we moved into an upper duplex unit on Twenty-third Avenue overlooking Milwaukee Avenue, I

A window reflection from 2012 Milwaukee Avenue reveals pre-renewal houses.

slowly gained the sense we were living in a neighborhood that resembled a small town.

The early 1970s continued the national penchant for all things new. Everyone's interest aimed to build the future. And this is what students were learning to do in architecture school at that time. This bias toward the new seemed perfectly explainable in the interest to get rid of the old—a sentiment that began in the post–World War II years. Architects teaching studio classes and my fellow students fervently believed we could "save the country" with new architecture. Unaware as architectural students were during this time, new buildings designed by architects' cult of the individual were paradoxically viewed by much of the public as a uniformity of structural design expressing emotional avoidance—incapable of human responses that could evoke delight.

But some of us were hearing Bob Dylan's admonition that the times were a' changing, and while his music undoubtedly contained several obscured references, one phrase might have portended a shift—that change could look backward as well as forward. Modernism held disdain for tradition as stultifying and nostalgia as superficial. Now came the entry of youth seeking to shake up societal values, to embrace patterns of the past as refreshing alternatives to modernism's long-standing delivery of an antiseptic aesthetic.

This shift became apparent in the early years of the 1970s, when several Minneapolis West Bank bars featured musicians adept in bluegrass fiddle music and blue-eyed, blond-haired guitar players offering renditions of the southern country blues by black musicians. A pair of country artists, Bill Hinkley and his wife, Judy Larson, became local favorites and lived in an older house in Seward West. On Milwaukee Avenue, two old homes that practically leaned on each other housed a musical collective that was transforming blues roots with rock rhythms into an updated genre that fit the sensibilities of this generation.

Soon enough, in the face of main media's obedience to presenting the next new, Garrison Keillor organized the KSJN public radio program, *The Prairie Home Companion*, which championed traditional cultural music performances mixed with Keillor-generated fictional characters who still lived in an era "that time forgot and the decades could not improve."

By this time, a few of us involved in architecture seemed unaware that the so-called modern movement had played itself out into designing buildings that were caricatures of one another. While that was happening on architects' drawing boards, the continuing loss of older, once-elegant-but-still-eye-catching buildings by the acts of federal bulldozers sparked public indignation by cadres of citizens who sought to disbelieve the perennial saying that "you can't beat city hall." Coincidentally, at this moment, a few quiet enclaves of historians began to see their field of history as too detached from the very historical movement of this time. History stepped in and sparked a catalytic moment that forged a stop-loss of urban architecture with newly discovered historic imperative. Historic preservation as a modern vital mechanism came into being.

Jeri remembers Annette Martin, who was in her eighties and had emigrated alone from Denmark at age fifteen. Annette and her family landed in Seward West when their farm in Wisconsin failed. Surely she could appreciate the tangle of vegetable gardens that the "hippie" families were planting on every scrap of land in the neighborhood. Their voluntary poverty must not have looked that much different from the involuntary poverty with which she was intimate.

By means of strategic political maneuvering, PAC eventually succeeded. PAC had imagination, but the Minneapolis Housing and Redevelopment Authority (HRA)—basically a land assembly program with zoning attached—did not. But perhaps the overall reason for PAC's success was that time had swept us into place, defined by a convergence spirit of the time—a zeitgeist. The ethic of activism seemed everywhere in our neighborhood, as if it was in the air all around us. We told ourselves our youthful idealism could save the country.

Eventually, the bounty of public funds, which was the result of the democratic effect of a large expanding economy and middle class, provided the financial and political means when the opportunity came to rebuild our neighborhood on our terms. Another part of the convergence was that history was changing, moving away from grand themes and eminent people to social history—the history of the common people in uncommon situations.

CHAPTER 1

Early City Land Patterns

I n the 1860s, early surveyors of Minneapolis followed the ubiquitous practice of American city development, using the grid system on the relatively flat land of the city and providing rectangular lots that benefitted the economical cost of building houses. Generally, this Minneapolis grid gave residential blocks a north–south length twice that of the east–west dimension, aiding address numbering and orientation. Establishing downtown's location in the center of the grid network gave proper perspective to the future city. Its skewed street layout on both sides of the Mississippi River near Saint Anthony Falls occurred before the greater north–south grid was planned. The grid's regularity was relieved by interruptions of public buildings, lakes, parks and occasional digressions of topography.

Residential lots in nineteenth- and early twentieth-century Minneapolis typically oriented their narrow sides to the streets, with the length of the lots running perpendicularly. This lot configuration, with narrow street frontages, offered several practical and economic considerations. In the given length of a city block, many more houses with street exposure could be built than if the lots were wider and shallower. This configuration facilitated predictable street patterns and public orientation, resulting in residential land acreage being more compact. It also made streetcar transportation more efficient by giving more ridership. The network provided accessible travel to downtown, work, shops, schools and places of worship. In south Minneapolis, the insistently repeating grid received a major digression in the form of the diagonally paired Hiawatha Avenue and Minnehaha Avenue, which flanked major railroad trackage of the Chicago, Milwaukee, St. Paul and Pacific Railroad, commonly called the Milwaukee Road. (Milwaukee takes its name from the river "Meneawkee" or "Mahnawaukee," which had been the site of an Indian village where the city in Wisconsin is now located.) This Minneapolis corridor followed a much earlier trail carved by Native Americans who traversed this area between two important sites: what became known as Saint Anthony Falls and the promontory above the joining of two great rivers: the Minnesota and Mississippi (below Fort Snelling). This railroad and street layout became important for the industrial development upon which Minneapolis was to grow.

Minneapolis's rapid industrial expansion between 1860 and the late 1880s resulted in a population growth from 3,000 to more than 164,000 during that thirty-year period. Industries and nearby residential settlement took advantage of mostly open and inexpensive land outside the downtown city core. In south Minneapolis, the need emerged for housing to accommodate the large number of factory and shop workers' families. Working-class neighborhoods formed near flour mills and nearby factories, railroad shop buildings and switching yards along railroad trackage in the Hiawatha/ Minnehaha industrial corridor.

The urban expansion that formed Minneapolis bore marked differences from many gargantuan metropolises in the eastern part of the nation. Urban historians have observed that in the second half of the nineteenth century, the nation's city life, powered by industrialization, changed more dramatically than it did during the Renaissance. In the east, railroads and associated resources amassed large-scale urban development, drawing large numbers of workers from rural areas and small towns, as well as unprecedented emigration from Europe. Cities built high-density housing in the form of apartment buildings, producing crowded tenements and resulting in low standards of decency and disease. By contrast, the founding of Minneapolis and nearby St. Paul was principally based on the mid-nineteenth-century industrial revolution, which gave the common population access to technological innovation.[1] Machine-cut lumber and housing components made building a home a viable option for those in the working class. As a result, early residential development occurred in the form of wood-framed houses on typical city lots. The craft of carpentry, which became the skill set of the working class, allowed these working-class houses to proliferate rapidly. As both Minneapolis and St. Paul were in their early growth at this time, expansive land areas of houses formed the predominant characteristic found in these cities today.

Throughout the 1870s and 1880s, land was sold off, subdivided and platted well beyond the current market, largely projected on rampant speculation. As a result, credit and land development became overextended, and the later Panic of 1893 caught many investors by surprise. Minneapolis had its share of big speculators during the boomtime preceding the 1893 panic, but the resultant downturn in land prices proved somewhat beneficial for small developers who concentrated on small parts of the city. The lower land costs also allowed those in the working class to buy or build their own homes.[2] Lower prices also resulted in single-family homes becoming economically viable, whereas many eastern cities saw high land values result in a preponderance of multi-unit structures. This might account for the lack of apartment buildings in Seward West (as well as in most parts of south Minneapolis) and the proliferation of single-family homes in the area. More importantly, this may have been a deciding factor in real estate speculator William Ragan buying the two blocks of land on which Milwaukee Avenue was to be located. Small single-family houses constructed on re-platted narrow lots could potentially provide Ragan with a much larger investment return.

It Started in the Alley

Milwaukee Avenue began as an alley, as evidenced by the original land plat created for the general area in the early 1880s. Jeri Reilly researched the origins of the avenue in a paper for a University of Minnesota history class. Her paper, titled "Temporary Home: The Immigrant in Minneapolis, 1895–1910 (Milwaukee Avenue: A Case Study)," notes:

> *The first house on Milwaukee Avenue was built in 1884, and most of the other homes were completed by 1890. The houses were built along what was intended to be an alley. And until 1906, the alley-street was officially named 22½ Avenue. Why the name was changed to Milwaukee Avenue remains unclear. The elderly residents in the neighborhood in the 1970s claim the houses were built either for or by the railroad workers who were employed in the nearby Chicago, Milwaukee, Saint Paul and Pacific Railroad car shops, commonly referred to as the "Milwaukee Road." However, in 1906, the residents of 22½ Avenue petitioned the City Council to have the name of the street changed, not to Milwaukee Avenue but to Woodland Avenue. Apparently a stigma was attached to the*

An old photograph of August Koch, a railroad conductor who lived on Milwaukee Avenue.

narrow street, for the petitioners stated, "We find the '½' objectional [sic] in speaking of it or writing letters. The '½' giving the impression that we live in an alley. And we think 'Woodland Ave' is more in keeping with the progression of Minneapolis than the 'Half Ave.'" Although elderly residents stick to their story that the houses along Milwaukee Avenue were associated with the railroad, no corroborative evidence has been found.

The name "Woodland Avenue" was never used, and the reason for the name change to Milwaukee Avenue is unknown. By that time, the preponderance of railroad workers, who worked in the nearby Milwaukee Railroad yards and lived on or near the street, might have led local residents to use the common reference of Milwaukee Avenue, it later becoming an official name.

Reilly's paper also describes the origins of the Milwaukee Avenue houses and how their lots were platted:

The majority of the houses on Milwaukee Avenue north of East 22nd Street were originally owned and built by a real estate agent, William Ragan, who, according to city directories, arrived in Minneapolis shortly before he purchased and platted the street and who left the city soon after foreclosure action had confiscated his property on 22½ Avenue. There was a great depression going on in the decade before 1900, and many others like Mr. Ragan fell into pecuniary disgrace. Back in 1884, however, William Ragan, who had a penchant for gambling, according to neighborhood legend, was somewhat less than modest in his approach to economic ventures. "Ragan's Addition to Minneapolis," as it was originally platted, composed two full blocks and two ¾ size blocks. In order to increase the development potential of his parcel, Ragan divided the land into four half-blocks. The alley between 22nd and 23rd Avenues was transformed into a street by taking 38 feet from the east face of the short lots on Blocks 1 and 2 of Ragan's Addition. Ragan went further. The lots he platted, already diminutive lengthwise because of the street easement, were measured in widths of only 25 feet (later increased to approximately 35 feet), about half the normal size of a city lot at that time. As a result of Ragan's intensive use of the land, the 46 single-family and duplex houses which line Milwaukee Avenue are extremely close together and have little, if any, setback from the sidewalk. It is apparent that such lot dissection was an attempt to increase the economic return on the land by building clusters of modest houses on small narrow lots.

Although Ragan sold many unimproved lots to individual contractors, most of the houses he himself contracted to build. It is easy to discern the Ragan-genre houses from the others, for he used the same house plan for each that he built. The typical Milwaukee Avenue house, the brick veneer single-family 1¾ story house with a front porch, is the design Ragan repeated one after another on the northeast block and that occurs less often on the other three blocks. The use of one house plan was certainly another device used by Ragan to reduce the amount of his investment.

The social and economic conditions which prevailed at that time complemented, if not stimulated, William Ragan's exploitation of the land. During the decade between 1880 and 1890, Minneapolis experienced a prodigious population increase. It was a boom time. And the burgeoning population contained increasing numbers of immigrants who needed low-cost housing during their first years in Minnesota. According to Hulda Anderson Marsh, who was born on 22½ Avenue in 1899, the daughter

A street view of brick duplexes at 2218, 2300, 2304 and 2308 Milwaukee Avenue gives a pre-renewal glimpse of the neighborhood.

of Swedish immigrant Otto Anderson, rental housing suitable for families was in short supply. The Anderson family of eight rented a house on 22½ Avenue despite its severe spatial limitations because it was the only low-cost rental housing they could find.

Ragan's sole objective was to increase return on his investment. He was undoubtedly unaware that one hundred years later, his venture would form a historic district, with its original re-platted land-use pattern directly transferable to an innovative, pedestrian-friendly living environment, reaching real estate values well beyond his dreams.

By the 1880s, along Franklin Avenue east of Minnehaha and Hiawatha Avenues, retail and service shops, saloons and churches served the basic needs of the nearby residents. People on the low end of the working-class scale made up a large portion of the population profile. Early owners and occupants of houses on Milwaukee Avenue and the surrounding neighborhood were people who struggled with the recurring economic vicissitudes of the late nineteenth- and early twentieth-century period. Throughout most of the twentieth century, families in this area bonded with one another, creating a unique neighborhood atmosphere.

By the late 1950s, the neighborhood no longer consisted entirely of older, longtime residents and their offspring. For many of these houses, their real estate value had little importance, as they had served only as hand-me-downs for the families and their nearby offspring. The increasing number of rental units in converted duplexes brought in more low-income people. By the 1960s, the area had become worn out, as neighborhoods close to the city core, inconsistent with suburban growth, were gradually left behind in the nation's tendency to continually retool itself.

In the early 1960s, the University of Minnesota began to expand across the Mississippi River to the West Bank. During that time, students were also seeking out the bar scene in that area, where drinks were cheap. Musicians, artists, poets and professors soon followed. The intelligentsia, themselves recently arrived, soon absorbed the emerging counterculture and likeminded young population.

Meanwhile, the second- and third-generation Swedes, Germans and Bohemians, whose ancestors arrived on the West Bank (well before it was given that name) in large numbers in the late 1800s, were leaving the many local bars early, before the arrival of the college crowd. The bar owners, seeking ways in which to keep the new customers in the bars longer, replaced the jukeboxes with the ready supply of local musicians, as well as drink specials. In 1963, locally renowned folk musician Maury Bernstein started to bring his accordion to the Triangle Bar on Riverside Avenue, gradually making that place a haven for emerging young folk musicians. John Koerner, Tony Clover and Dave Ray, all of whom later received national recognition, were among the many musicians who found this the ideal setting in which to incorporate rock influences in their music.

By the early 1970s, Cedar Avenue businesses had taken on San Francisco retail characteristics, such as fern bars, Marimekko fabric and pottery stores, restaurants with international cuisines and serious music and drama stages. Various protesters and the hippie culture found the West Bank to be a perfect base, and their activities gave the area a certain notoriety. The counterculture and students seeking cheap rent found nearby areas with run-down older houses that gave an ambience of certain appeal. By 1974, nearby Twenty-second Avenue South and Milwaukee Avenue had become the place to be. Blues musicians Dave Ray and Willie Murphy lived in side-by-side houses on Milwaukee Avenue, along with techie Steve Raitt, whose sister Bonnie stopped by once in a while to send blues from their front porches out into the street.

In late autumn, the tree branches are bare and the intricate totality of Milwaukee Avenue's porches becomes more noticeable.

Reilly points out how, just like its first residents, this second wave of immigrants to Seward West, especially in the four blocks around Milwaukee Avenue, settled the neighborhood based on its affordability. Oddly enough, many of these young people bore certain resemblances to the early inhabitants. The hippies wore workmen's clothing such as plaid shirts and service jackets with oval name labels over the left pocket, long skirts, boots and wire-rimmed glasses. They also used yard space for planting vegetable gardens and did not consider lawn care a priority. These people also considered their dwelling places as temporary. A major difference was that the early residents' frugal lives were determined by economic necessity, whereas many of the 1970s generation chose a voluntary poverty—which public agency staff member Bob Scroggins called "conspicuous non-consumption." The hippies electively chose what the older residents had assumed was how living was supposed to happen. Non-conspicuous minimal consumption could describe the mix of older longtime residents and their younger offspring, who lived in acceptable union with the hippies and people of similar predilection.

In 1970, the Minneapolis Housing and Redevelopment Authority declared the thirty-five-block area in the western part of Seward as a renewal area. The Seward West Urban Renewal Plan mandated demolition of 70 percent of the area's houses, including all forty-six houses facing Milwaukee Avenue.

CHAPTER 2

Milwaukee Avenue:
The Street, Its Houses and Its Landscape

LILACS, ELM TREES AND WIRE FENCES

Part of the wonderful character of pre-renewal Milwaukee Avenue were the thick-trunked, tall elm trees, mostly on its west side, whose spreading branches gave a lofty canopy above the narrow street. Unruly branches of smaller trees in the yards between and in the rear of the houses were pleasantly interrupted by clumps of lilacs in the spring, spraying their fragrant, pale blue-lavender blossoms over rickety wire fences along Milwaukee Avenue's sidewalks, often causing passersby to bend down a bit or walk around them. Today, much of that character is still in place, minus the old wire fences.

In backyards, hollyhocks stood proud around chicken-wire racks that allowed clematis and sweet pea plants to tangle upward for the several widows living on Milwaukee Avenue, Twenty-second Avenue and Twenty-third Avenue. Most of the backyards' very small spaces had coarse patches of grass or bare ground, but occasional flowerbeds of petunias, pansies and various annuals offered tiny arrangements of summer color. When hippies came to live here in the early 1970s, this landscape disorder provided exactly the environment they wanted. Vegetable gardens took over many backyards, some of them bordered with tall cornstalks to block public view of their crop of choice.

THE STREET

Milwaukee Avenue lived throughout its pre-renewal existence as a 26-foot-wide north–south asphalt street, bordered on each side by approximately 4-foot-wide boulevards and 5-foot-wide sidewalks. The houses were built 1 foot or so from the sidewalks. Its approximately 1,400 feet in length, from

An evening street view of typical workman's cottages on Milwaukee Avenue before renewal.

Milwaukee Avenue's linear composure can be enhanced by the colors of autumn.

Franklin Avenue to East Twenty-fourth Street, intersected East Twenty-second Street at its midpoint. Automobile traffic was one-way, southward, with curbside parking on the east side. But by far its greatest use was pedestrian traffic—people on foot or on bicycles who used the street with great frequency. Its asphalt surface bore a succession of numerous patch jobs, giving it a bumpy and irregular surface.

The street's narrowness brought the faces of the houses and their porches on both sides of the street much closer together, especially with almost all of the houses having practically no front yards (most of them had only a strip of property wide enough to service their front steps). The modest size of the houses and the meager yard space between them is what created Milwaukee Avenue's unique character.

Balance without Symmetry

At the beginning of the urban renewal program in Seward West, thirty-four of the forty-six houses facing Milwaukee Avenue were single-unit dwellings, and fourteen structures were duplexes with one-bedroom units (two since converted to single-unit houses). There were two fourplexes at the very southern end facing East Twenty-fourth Street, one of which was demolished and replaced by a six-unit side-by-side town house and the other rehabilitated into three side-by-side town houses facing Milwaukee Avenue.

The typical Milwaukee Avenue one-and-three-quarter-story house is a study in architectural composition, serving as both a singular element and as a contributor to the streetscape. The home's narrow profile is given proper proportion with its height, as a taller height would overstate its narrow street façade. Proportion, defined as the mathematical relationship between the parts of the whole, is further established by the pair of narrow arched head windows, whose narrowness is compensated for by their centered location within the triangulation of the gable face, which would otherwise be diminished within a normal full second-story wall. This simplicity of the upper façade is a critical factor when viewed in combination with other houses, as these upper elements, uncomplicated by detail, allow the tightly repetitive rooftops to form a rhythmic pattern. This pattern, the strongest component of the streetscape, is given uniformity by the nearly exact rooftop heights of the houses.

But the porches at eye level subtly contrast the gables. Queen Anne–influenced ornamentation supplies insistent repetition of lathe-turned

This circa 1973 view of Milwaukee Avenue depicts typical pre-renewal workman's cottages.

The workman's cottages have elaborate gable triangular panels that reinforce the architectural continuity of the houses along Milwaukee Avenue.

This close-up view of a workman's cottage porch shows complex detail balanced by the simplicity of the house's architecture, a sight that becomes amplified by the collective view of the houses aligned on the street.

columns, between which are fine-grained details such as brackets, spindle rows and spandrels with filigree infill, whose arched shapes with classic curving profiles reinforce the lacy continuity of the street's architecture. Thus, complexity does happen in a vernacular residential district built for factory worker families. This is remarkable because the aforementioned architectural qualities are usually reserved for mid- and high-bracket urban environments.

Brick is typically not used for worker houses, but that material seems to dominate Milwaukee Avenue. Both the original and replacement bricks are made of a soft, low-fired clay and are mostly beige with varying yellowish or faint orange tones. The clay for the original bricks was excavated from the banks of the Mississippi River in north Minneapolis. Three houses were clad with red brick, called St. Louis brick.

Viewing the street from its northern end near Franklin Avenue, the left-hand (east) side presents the typical one-and-three-quarter-story brick homes in alignment until the street's end at East Twenty-fourth Street. These east-side houses, built with nearly identical designs that somehow defy standardization, form a highly representative image of Milwaukee Avenue.

This east-side view of the street looks north toward pre-renewal Franklin Avenue. All but two houses in this image were rehabilitated.

This pre-renewal photo of 2012 Milwaukee Avenue depicts one of ten wood-sided houses on the street.

As if to enhance this continuity, the builders of these houses set the threshold heights of nearly every house on this side of the street at the same horizontal elevation, even though the grade slopes slightly downward (approximately three feet) from Franklin Avenue to East Twenty-fourth Street.

Early construction on these houses occurred with an apparent lack of a deliberate overall development plan. The structures on the west side of the street do not replicate the fine-grained detail and close-order repetition of the east-side houses but instead serve the whole architectural composition by providing a slight irregularity of roof heights (while in strict obedience with identical gable slopes) with accompanying porch details and slightly varying façade designs. Approximately half of the houses are brick; the others are clad in narrow-lap wood siding.

A sense of balance rather than strict equilateral symmetry is one of the many factors that endow the street with its unique and piquant character. The overall architectural composition would be less interesting with an equilateral streetscape. Although houses along the east side have consistent one-and-three-quarter-story massing, the west-side houses vary in clusters from one and three-quarters stories to two and a half stories in height. Just as with works of art, unequal proportion can sometimes achieve a sense of balance, unaided by symmetry.

THE LANGUAGE OF ARCHITECTURE, THE STORIES OF HOUSES

Architecture, in aggregate on a large scale and depending on particular circumstances, can create a language when the need arises to reflect collective identity. Architectural scholar Anthony Alofsin notes that using language as a metaphor to describe architecture can be beneficial, as language is a vehicle of communication and establishes identity within a broader cultural context.[3] An architectural language derives from a more indirect base. But it is important to distinguish the language of architecture as separate from style, despite their seeming equivalency.

The term "style" can be readily applied to buildings possessing articulated features or ornamental elements that serve to identify the buildings' architecture as belonging to a body of similar structures with common characteristics produced within a culture in a defined period.[4] This form of architecture can be called "high style" and is associated with houses with extensive ornamentation and the upper economic class

The upper gable of 2012 Milwaukee Avenue presents a handsome composition of Victorian Stick features, such as simple strapwork of straight and curved members, segmental sunbursts at the lower ends and just enough scroll-cut filigree at the gable top to maintain a sense of simplicity for this vernacular structure.

vested in such buildings. By contrast, buildings purposed for everyday uses and marked by a more straightforward architectural design are commonly called "vernacular." Their architectural forms often develop from tradition-based uses and construction methods. The vernacular often arises from a broad base of building making and becomes a visual language. High-style architectural structures definitively belong to a style, while vernacular buildings typically belong to a "type" rather than a style. Vernacular buildings can tell us about their function and place in our working and cultural environments, as well as why they were created in the traditional patterns in which they were built, occasionally using minor references to their historical and social origins.

In vernacular architecture, traditional houses achieve visual grace when a limited amount of ornamental detail is placed where it is most appealing to the eye. The ornament comes from whatever style or fragments of styles the builder is accustomed to working with. "This is what makes vernacular buildings so interesting," comments architectural historian Anders Christensen. "The styles flow into each other, producing unlikely combinations of elements that while not 'correct' can be very pleasing."[5]

This brings up the following question, which paraphrases architectural writer Witold Rybczynski: Was this whole ensemble of houses and street created by a designer with a broad vision, enigmatically perceiving how to form a unique sense of city life in the time of its making, possessing an unusual talent in composing buildings in relation and proportion to one another in a setting that could enhance the lives of those inhabitants and the well being of the city?[6]

The answer seems to be the simple realization that Milwaukee Avenue was primarily built as a means to follow the money. Real estate speculator William Ragan doubled his initial investment by re-platting the lots into smaller parcels, revised the original alley into a narrow street and placed houses right up to the street, with no front yards. We can only assume that what appears to be a creative formation was set in place by serendipity following the money.

Milwaukee Avenue was part of a much larger pattern of speculative building in south Minneapolis.[7] A significant aspect is that many, if not all, of the vernacular small worker cottages in the central part of nineteenth-century Minneapolis are anonymous in physical presence and seem to possess minimal architectural character. In this context, the Milwaukee Avenue houses are anomalies. They are mostly brick, whereas very few workers' houses are, and despite having no discernable architectural style, they possess a seemingly perfect pitch of proportion of elements, with more articulated ornamental detail than most vernacular examples.

Ragan's choice of brick for the houses' exterior material and his relative lack of restraint in the degree of ornamental features seems to counter the notion that he was just in this for the money, as brick and ornamentation undoubtedly increased construction costs. So why did William Regan build these houses with the grace and architectural quality they possess? The answer, unfortunately, might forever remain unanswered.

HOUSE PLANS

Almost every working-class neighborhood in south Minneapolis has dwellings derived from the minds of carpenters and from house-plan catalogues. The western part of Seward is no exception. It is not known where the builders of the Milwaukee Avenue houses obtained their house plans. It may be assumed that, in the greater part of Seward West, houses were built by local tradesmen who usually constructed only one at a time by using plans they were familiar with and available materials purchased from nearby suppliers.

What about the plans themselves? The phrase "plan in the head" was a familiar one throughout most of the nineteenth century—a time in America when building domestic shelter took place mostly in rural areas, on farms or in small villages, by cutting lumber directly from fallen trees and then hand-sawing it into members and pegging them into place. The variety of design forms was limited, and the need for paper plans was unnecessary. By the 1880s, however, after the introduction of industrialized lumber, printing technology made possible plan books for realtors and house builders. These books featured floor plans and sketch views of a wide variety of houses, initially influenced by the Victorian Stick and, later, Foursquare Prairie vernacular styles.

However, these houses are different from other nearby structures in many respects. The floor plan for a typical Milwaukee Avenue house does not appear anywhere else in the surrounding area. Brick as a cladding material used as consistently and on houses this small does not appear elsewhere in the neighborhood or the city, especially when combined with the use of ornamental elements and front gable tracery at the front gable peak, which are likewise absent. Unfortunately, there are no known records of how these houses were constructed. In this way, Milwaukee Avenue houses, as well as the street on which they are aligned, represent a curious exception within Minneapolis vernacular architecture.

CHAPTER 3
Construction and Function

All of the houses along Milwaukee Avenue are designed in the typical box shape with identical twelve-foot by twelve-foot roof pitches, signifying a simple construction formula that compares horizontal length to vertical height. Twenty houses on the east side of the street and two on the west side can be classified as workman's cottages, all of them brick and having nearly identical architectural shapes and features. The main body of the typical one-and-three-quarter-story single-unit house has a one-story rear section that contains the kitchen and an enclosed rear/side porch. The kitchen's width juts out approximately one and a half feet at one sidewall and continues along that wall to form a shallow one-story extension for a narrow bedroom.

The front porch extends nearly across the width of the façade. These porches have mansard-type roofs (a nearly flat roof surface with steeply sloping faces on the porch roof's sides and front). The porch roof is supported by a horizontal beam and four lathe-turned wood columns approximately four and a half inches in diameter and is given lateral reinforcement by spindlework friezes—bands of lathe-turned wood spindles spaced a few inches apart and connected vertically to horizontal wood strips just under the roof beam and between the columns. Just below the spindle frieze, arched spandrels with scroll-cut curvilinear patterns attach to the underside of the spindle frieze and against the sides of columns. These style elements—Mansard roofs, spindle friezes and arched spandrels—occur occasionally on Queen Anne–style houses in several urban neighborhoods, lending these houses their only identifiable style details, which are sparse in quantity but effectively located for aesthetics.

A total of twenty-nine of the Milwaukee Avenue houses are clad in brick in a method known as veneer cladding, in which a single brick wythe (an Old English term still in use in today's construction vernacular) covers the main wood framing. These houses originally had limestone foundations that extended little more than two feet into the ground, with the limestone thick enough to form a masonry ledge to support the brick veneer. Floor joists, two feet by eight feet in size, at both floors run as continuous members from one side to the other and are sheathed with one-inch-thick boards set diagonally for added reinforcement. These boards were typically ten to twelve inches wide, but some were as wide as twenty-six inches, having been cut from large trees in old-growth northern Minnesota forests. The walls utilized "balloon framing," which extended two-by-fours from the first floor up along and above the second-floor walls to support the roof framing. The top height of the sidewalls is approximately six feet above the second floor; sloping roof rafters formed two feet of sloped ceiling at both sides of the flat ceiling surface of the second-floor rooms.

The original interior floor plan was very simple, designed for ultimate function within the house's width—which varies from eighteen feet in the front section to twenty feet in the main section—and some measure of comfort (as much as the small floor plans could allow). The front entrance gives entry to a narrow hallway, also serving as a stairwell leading to the second floor. A doorway off to one side of the hallway opens to the parlor, or living room, and a doorway straight ahead leads to the dining room, which is larger than the parlor. Located at one side of the dining room is a seven-foot- by twelve-foot bedroom, commonly known as the mother-in-law bedroom. A doorway located off-center on the dining room's rear wall gives entry to the kitchen and access to the side porch. The second floor typically contains two bedrooms, each with one small closet, and a bathroom. Most of these second-floor bathrooms were added a number of years after original construction when outdoor toilets were no longer in vogue.

Very few of the houses had full basements. Usually a small, low-ceilinged cellar could be accessed by a steep stairway under the main stairs. A large, round brick-walled cistern was typically inserted into this underground area below the kitchen, accessed by a very narrow passageway from the cellar.

The larger two-story duplex structures on the west side of Milwaukee Avenue, as well as those duplexes behind them on Twenty-second Avenue, had similar original floor plans and exterior architectural forms but were later revised during rehabilitation. This pre-renewal street frontage consisted of thirty houses, approximately half of them duplexes. Most of the houses on Twenty-third Avenue were wood- or stucco-covered one-story structures with varied floor plans, and most of them were much smaller than typical neighborhood houses. This street frontage had a total of twenty houses in pre-renewal time, but several in the southern block between East Twenty-second Street and East Twenty-fourth Street were too small to be functional living units and were extremely dilapidated. Today, eleven Twenty-third Avenue dwellings remain.

PHYSICAL CONDITIONS IN THE PRE-RENEWAL ERA

By 1970, the houses along Milwaukee Avenue, having originally been built as cheap housing with somewhat less than average quality construction methods and inhabited by generations of households with meager means for maintenance and repair, had reached significant levels of deterioration.

An interior view of a second-floor bedroom in a typical Milwaukee Avenue workman's cottage.

Roof shingles were worn out, and much of the original brick had long ago been covered with stucco to fill in cracks. Windows and doors were worn and damaged, and the houses' original ornamental porches had long ago collapsed or were nearing collapse, shabbily closed in with wall framing and storm windows, with their ornamental features removed. Many of the interior rooms had cracked plaster and/or cheap, thin wood paneling over missing plaster; wood trim with many coats of paint; and window curtains in great need of repair. Almost all of the houses had thirty-amp electrical service, barely functioning bathrooms and space heaters in lieu of central heat.

As the houses aged, they experienced many changes. Their successive owners altered their homes according to their personal needs and the inevitable needs of household budgets, maintenance and repair. Architectural correctness was not a part of their thinking. Replacing original windows with lumberyard sizes could be accomplished by placing plywood between the window frame and the surrounding brick wall, and asphalt roofing shingles seemed adequate substitutes for the original cedar shingles.

THE EVENTUAL RESULT

Of the forty-six houses facing Milwaukee Avenue at the outset of renewal, twenty of the twenty-seven single-unit houses, ten duplexes and one fourplex were rehabilitated; eight Milwaukee Avenue houses were demolished during the 1970s revitalization. New single-unit replicas replaced six of those demolished houses. The overall result was that 82 percent of the original houses facing Milwaukee Avenue were saved, as were 62 percent of the houses in the four-block area on Twenty-second and Twenty-third Avenues and East Twenty-fourth Street. The 1970s rehabilitation process altered all of these houses' interior spaces, some slightly and others extensively.

The survival and resurrection of these structures can adequately be described as their being in the right place at the right time. But another factor might be at play here. Each house's role as contributing to an ensemble has been previously noted. To this point, their historic designation has been noted in terms of their being part of a district rather than each having individual historic merit. But it might be instructive to examine how these houses of vernacular beginnings possess the perfect pitch of residential design in context of its purpose. Aside from this vernacular language, there are the stories. In the pre-renewal days, Milwaukee Avenue houses told us stories.

Throughout the first part of their history, the prime function of these structures was serving as dwellings in which successions of households lived their lives, often in the most basic circumstances. These people lived their lives by stories that measured who they were, and layers of stories became the compound interest of invested lives. When these houses were emptied of the succession of their inhabitants, those stories somehow remained. Walking past these houses gave us, as if with psychic imprint on their walls, a sense that they could tell us stories—not in a particular or literal sense, but in a sense that they could somehow evoke feelings and impressions. Jeri remembers sorting through a vacant house's attic and spying a stylish wool women's jacket that bespoke of the middle-class life associated with it, and nearby was a diary written in the years of World War I—stories just asking to be read. One morning, Jeri and I were surveying a vacant house at 2215 Milwaukee to record its condition, and while she was talking to me about such details, it was difficult for me to pay attention to her; instead, I was absorbed by the strong sense that I could feel the people from long ago and what they were doing at an undefined instance of time now so long forgotten.

CHAPTER 4
Transformation Begins

During the late 1960s and early '70s, the Vietnam War had become the most prevailing issue among college-age young people. An outcome of this dubiously regarded conflict turned into massive opposition. Around the University of Minnesota campus, young college students and instructors exercised highly vocal tactics and physical confrontation in frequent street protests to challenge federal government authority. Helter-skelter actions formed a movement, a collective will that needed very little connective structure and became absorbed into the thinking, if not lifestyle, of young people, whether they were protesters or those generally sympathetic. Many mild-mannered young people had begun to wear buttons that displayed the now ubiquitous peace symbol, but the stickers and buttons that proclaimed "Question Authority" set in motion an attitude that began to affect certain minds outside of the prevailing antiwar sentiment. In fact, "Question Authority" became foremost in the minds of the emerging activists in a neighborhood known as Seward West, as a neighborhood-saving struggle was beginning to take shape.

Many longtime Seward West residents were or had been factory workers at nearby industries, and many of them had forbearers who had lived there in the neighborhood's early days. Some residents were retired from factory jobs due to reaching retirement age or from various injuries; others worked as custodians, nursing home aides, laundry workers and truck drivers; and still others were elderly residents who had retired long ago. Sprinkled into the neighborhood were young students taking advantage of inexpensive housing close to the university, Augsburg College and various nursing schools at nearby hospitals.

On Twenty-third Avenue, many households were interrelated, composed of residents who had lived in that same area of that avenue all their lives. Children who grew up there played together, went to school together and often married someone from a few houses away.

In 1970, the Minneapolis Housing and Redevelopment Authority (HRA) initiated the Seward West Renewal Program, which was approved by the Minneapolis City Council. The federal department of Housing and Urban Development (HUD) committed $5.2 million for program and operational expenses to HRA. The City of Minneapolis pledged infrastructure improvements such as new streets, a park, an elementary school connected to a community center, street repaving and underground utilities. HRA operational expenses included property acquisition, redevelopment assistance and other costs.

Seward West, as described in the HRA renewal plan, was a thirty-five-block area in the western part of the Seward neighborhood, bounded on the north by Interstate 94, the west by the railroad tracks just west of Minnehaha Avenue, the south by a line one block south of East Twenty-fourth Street and a generally irregular east boundary along the east side of Twenty-fifth Avenue South jogging two blocks to the east just south of East Twenty-fourth Street. HRA considered most of the approximately 535 houses in Seward West that were built as working-class housing to be inferior in construction to the middle-class houses in the eastern part of Seward. It further determined that many of these houses were deteriorated beyond rehabilitation, and the result was over that 70 percent of the houses were listed for demolition. As for the 46 houses facing Milwaukee Avenue, HRA slated all of them for razing. And to their alleged extremely decrepit condition, the agency added "planning reasons," namely their narrow lots and the fact that they did not have front yards.

An important funding component was the cost of relocation of residents, both homeowners and renters. Besides purchasing houses at a fair market value from homeowner-occupants, HRA was committed by HUD requirements to pay a relocation grant to these homeowners to assist their purchase of a house. (Absentee homeowners received purchase price only.)

As the program began, residents began receiving occasional letters from HRA. They began to worry about "having to sell our house to the government and having to move." These attempts to officially inform residents became the subject throughout the neighborhood of great misunderstanding, as HRA's bureaucratic language proved to be of little communication value to most Seward West homeowners, who instead relied on second-hand stories of previous urban renewal programs in which the government forced people out of their homes with minimal compensation. This misunderstanding turned into fear, as many Seward West residents had lived in the neighborhood all their lives, with generations of families living close to one another—often on the same street. Their knowledge of the greater city of Minneapolis was limited, and the bond of neighbors and relatives was strong and reassuring. The thought of having to move to some other area of the city was augmented by uncertainty.

"I DON'T WANT TO BE RENEWED!"

When men on the chessboard get up
And tell you where to go...
When logic and proportion have fallen sloppy dead
And the white knight is talking backwards.
—*Jefferson Airplane, "White Rabbit," 1967*

The introduction of the Seward West renewal process to the neighborhood came on a September evening in 1970. In the large gymnasium/multi-purpose room of the Matthews Community Center, many rows of folding chairs were filled with over one hundred Seward West residents, who faced a long table of Minneapolis HRA officials sitting on a platform. The purpose of the meeting was supposedly to update neighborhood residents on the urban renewal program that had recently begun operations. One by one, each of the officials took the microphone to explain his or her role in the process and recited some policies that basically amounted to strings of bureaucratic words the audience could not understand. When it came time for the audience to ask questions, one resident after another expressed confusion and uncertainty as to how long they could stay in their houses. Almost every audience member would end by asking, "Can you please tell me when will you buy my house and when will I have to move?" The invariably bureaucratic response from the officials was that the process was still being organized and that no timetable had been set. Still, the residents wanted specific information.

But many of these residents had their own agenda items. Some of the city officials had explained that the purpose of urban renewal was to eliminate "blighting conditions" from neighborhoods, further adding, in statistical terms, that many of the houses in Seward West were deteriorated and in need of demolishing. Those words—"purpose of urban renewal"—became repeated over and over and became a phrase wherein the officials could assign purpose to their words and, perhaps, also their work lives. When the homeowners heard these compiled numbers, they knew the statistics could be applied to the houses in which they were living and in which their parents had lived before them. Neighborhood homes were now being described as statistical entities—a quantity measured by public agency planners who probably had not seen the home nor been inside it to gain a sense of what made it special to its owners.

This undoubtedly accounted for the homeowners' occasional outbursts of anger that framed their defiance. One longtime resident ended his comments with a defiant declaration: "I don't want to be renewed!" One collage-age neighbor then asked, "What can you tell these residents that can guarantee that your program can keep them in their neighborhood?" The city staffer chairing the meeting gave a feigned grimace and then turned his head down the table and, in a fatigued voice, said, "Well, Gene, you'll have to answer that question one more time." And the response came slowly as it was read from a sheaf of papers: "The purpose of urban renewal..."

CUE THE PROTESTERS

The format of basic questions turned into an evening of active protest when a procession of mostly young people stepped up to the floor microphone. Many stated that the whole renewal program should be stopped. A U of M studio arts student shouted, "Their plan should be shoved into a waste basket!" This received a bit of applause. Many with strident voices made statements such as, "This is another event by government to force people into what the people don't want to do," which brought out repeated shouts of, "Question Authority!" Someone else in the crowd yelled, "You people are like the U.S. general in Vietnam who stated his troops had to destroy a village in order to save it, and you want to save this neighborhood by bulldozing it!" This drew much applause and more shouting. Did these people subconsciously sense that they were in the here-and-now wonderland of Alice, where, right in front of their eyes, Gracie Slick and Jefferson Airplane seemed to be telling them that "logic and proportion have fallen sloppy dead. And the white knight is talking backwards."

But who could ask Alice?

Then a young man who identified himself as Tony Scallon, a schoolteacher, stepped up and said, "There's a few houses over there on Twenty-fourth Avenue that seem in good shape, and then there is this nice duplex on East Twenty-second Street that just got painted." He then made several remarks about particular technical references in HRA's manual used to administer its program and, raising his voice considerably, expertly challenged the officials in detail, point by point. More important, however, was the fact that his words seemed to raise the energy level of this section of the crowd. Tony indicated that opposition must be formed and that those interested should gather together outside the building after the meeting.

Neighborhood Politics—1970s Style

There's something happening here
What it is ain't exactly clear.
—*Buffalo Springfield, "For What It's Worth," 1966*

Sometime later, a loosely organized neighborhood meeting dealt with the upcoming Seward West urban renewal issue, about which many residents knew practically nothing. The scene was unlike what a neighborhood meeting should be, where decorum and defined procedure would be the order of the evening. To the assembled crowd, various speakers projected their anti–public agency attitudes, delivered in strong words streaked with anger. Most of the speakers were young men and women clothed in well-worn plaid shirts and floppy jeans, with long hair as unruly as their rhetoric. The most provocatively resplendent of these speakers was Jack Cann, whose lower-class speaking manner masked his brilliant mind as he pungently carried an articulate bombast castigating the insensitivity of government's neighborhood renewal policies that degraded the people it intended to serve.

As things progressed, Buffalo Springfield's lyrics from a few years before, as written by Stephen Stills, seemed to tell the crowd the situation. People's consciousnesses were exactly clear. They knew what was happening here: the now-familiar antiwar confrontations on downtown streets and college campuses were being brought into the Seward West neighborhood. Defiance was replacing compliance. Urban renewal was the new citizens' war.

When Seward West activists later evolved into organized opposition, their cause readily adapted the spirit of antiwar rhetoric, but the tactics became very different. Instead of flamboyant public protest events, the neighborhood activists chose strident, face-to-face and, often, strong-voiced confrontations in meetings with public agency staff. They studied the minutiae of renewal policy very carefully in order to better deal with these staffers on their own terms. While the public agency officials had to learn everything in their thick urban renewal manuals, the activists zeroed in on the more pertinent regulations, allowing them to reference these issues better than the planners.

Other speakers expressed variations of Jack's message, but a few residents became particularly attracted to the quieter but determined voice of Peter Hall, a Minneapolis architect and one of the city's earliest voices in the need to save older buildings, presaging the soon-to-come historic preservation movement in the city. His words departed from the social and political imperatives and instead articulated his message that, from an architectural point of view, saving older buildings was important. Until now, creativity had focused exclusively on the design of new buildings. But the main principle behind Hall's approach could be put into a phrase new to many: "adaptive reuse," the concept of discovering how new uses could fit appropriately in older buildings. Adaptive reuse was what Hall had recently accomplished with his new trendsetting restaurant, Pracna, which was housed in an old, once-abandoned building on a largely empty street. The bumpy street with misshapen granite pavers later became Saint Anthony Main, and the old 1860s and 1870s warehouse buildings lining the street eventually became trendy shops and restaurants. He ended his speech by stating that one of Seward West's hidden streets, Milwaukee Avenue, had many examples of older architecture that should be saved for their historical significance.

CHAPTER 5
Urban Renewal and Its Discontents

We all want to change the world,
But when you talk about destruction,
Don't you know you can count me out.
—The Beatles, "Revolution"

On April 13, 1933, President Franklin D. Roosevelt promoted passage of the Home Owners Loan Corporation (HOLC), whose effect was providing long-term, self-amortizing uniform payments extending over the life of the debt. For the first time, average homebuyers had dependability and certainty in a streamlined and predictable process. In itself, this process greatly aided most Americans. However, certain pervasive practices became part of HOLC. Redlining by banks developed as a means to rate neighborhoods in a way that undervalued them according to density, race or the number of aging homes, as noted by Kenneth T. Jackson in his 1987 publication *Crabgrass Frontier.*

Homogeneity increasingly became the measuring stick, dubiously denoting infiltration of Jews and racial members. Socioeconomic characteristics of a neighborhood determined the value of housing to a greater extent than physical condition. The ultimate result was downgraded real estate values in central cities, which eventually augmented ongoing deterioration, absentee ownership and many other factors and shifted housing investment from cities to suburbs.

The Federal Housing Administration (FHA) was organized in 1934 as a means to stimulate housing construction outside of the government by relying on private enterprise to insure home mortgages backed with government guarantees. Another objective was to devise the housing standards, later to be called "FHA standards," required to gain FHA approval. In 1939, FHA promulgated brochures for "Typical American Houses" depicting bungalows or Colonials on generous lots and promoting the national aspiration toward suburban living. Minimum lot sizes were established, as was the minimum width for a house and distance at which it had to be set back from the street.

Rehabilitation of existing homes and high-density attached housing was not eligible for FHA or VA residential loan policies. The result was that only low-density suburban federally insured loans were issued during the time when the nation built a substantial volume of its housing stock, producing a highly transformative effect on the American landscape.[8] FHA's mortgage underwriting policies had widespread effects beyond home financing. Jackson noted that the federal role in the domestic land-use regulations was immense and far reaching, as the government's transportation policy served mainly to promote the automobile, which had a pervasive impact on Americans in the half century between 1934 and 1984.

Although various federal housing policies starting in the 1930s displayed many deliberate attitudes and actions skewed toward shifting housing development away from cities, racial factors were judged as inadvertent. Not so with the FHA. Jackson's book presents a multitude of policies intended to inhibit approved mortgages to "all-Negro" applicants.[9] Whereas HOLC's intended favoritism toward homogenous suburbs had unintended racist outcomes, the overt racism of the FHA's policies tipped toward urban disinvestment, aggravated by additional factors such as the redlining of entire neighborhoods.[10] As a result, the residential construction industry became geared almost wholly to new houses and away from rehabilitation.

The World War II development of mass-produced ships, aircraft and other military infrastructure became quickly converted to postwar civilian fabrication processes for home construction. This factor, coupled with cheaper land costs, generated an unprecedented housing market. The public's newfound materialism seemed justified by returning military veterans fixated on their futures and the civilian workforce who had endured hardships working for the war effort. Now the older, prewar neighborhoods represented a history to be left behind.

The development of suburbs just outside city boundaries began in the late 1940s as readily available farm fields and meandering woodlands beckoned homebuilders and a war-weary public seeking a new future, which cities were no longer assumed to provide. New federally subsidized freeways brought them there. Strip malls and shopping centers, office parks, churches and schools soon followed. In 1945, only 1 percent of the nation's land was urbanized, where two-thirds of Americans lived.[11] New houses and new cars became the new standard. The suburban boom continued for nearly seventy years, eventually blunted by the mortgage fallout near the end of the first decade of the twenty-first century.

By the 1950s, many inner-city neighborhoods experienced a shift from owner-occupied dwellings to rental properties. Houses whose real estate values were declining were now owned by inattentive landlords and occupied by people with diminished means for repair. Over time, the decline in housing maintenance produced the resultant effect of visible deterioration, which began a cycle of reduced real estate values. This in turn reduced property taxes, shifting city assistance funding toward more stable neighborhoods. This segment of the housing market caused vacant homes to stand empty for months and longer, worsening the stability of these neighborhoods, perpetuating disrepair and stultifying the inner-city housing market. At this point, FHA declared it was "not in the business to help cities but to revive home building, stimulate homeownership and reduce unemployment. Its policies supported the income and racial segregation of the suburbs. Perhaps for the first time, the federal government embraced the discriminatory attitudes of the marketplace."[12]

The U.S. Congress and various federal departments were disinterested in the prejudicial practices of FHA until the 1960s civil rights movement and the rise of community groups began to point out how the act of redlining and the FHA were exacerbating urban decline. Urban observer and writer Jane Jacobs commented, "Credit blacklisting maps are accurate prophecies because they are self-fulfilling prophecies."[13] The FHA was induced to change its policies, but the net effect was to benefit white homeowners and contractors.

URBAN RENEWAL

As the phenomenon of suburbs hindered growth of cities, the federal government realized that the need for rebuilding distressed urban areas required a multifaceted analysis to address what could be a systematic remedial application. The affected multiple interests were widespread in public and private quarters, some at odds with others in the policy puzzle.

Many working-class neighborhoods around the core of the city became zoned for medium density, and urban renewal policies promoted "highest and best use." These areas were ripe for rezoning (part of typical urban renewal programs) to more economic (higher value) development. This eventually became the basis for PAC's strongly argued contention that the neighborhood's traditional homes would be torn down for new apartment buildings.

The formative beginnings of urban renewal can be traced back to pre-modern days, when national powers took on an expansive style of governance. The technological benefits of industrial revolution produced adverse effects in urban areas, such as the overcrowded conditions of nineteenth-century London, New York, Paris and other major cities.

In the United States, the design and construction of Central Park in New York and various City Beautiful vision projects by Daniel Burnham could be considered early urban renewal projects. Demolition of degraded areas of New York in the late nineteenth-century led to formative urban renewal programs.

The Housing Act of 1949 had, as its main preoccupation, the objective of slum clearance, which portended things to come. In 1954, the law was broadened into a program labeled as "Urban Renewal." Several goals emerged: attracting middle-class families and businesses back into the city, rebuilding slum areas, improving the quality of life, improving tax revenues and improving the real estate market.[14]

Early urban renewal efforts intended to produce new construction projects with the visual impact that could provide public presence of demonstrable change. This meant new buildings, as the public eye could understand quickly how new buildings symbolized the mission of urban renewal. These buildings served as functional urban amenities, such as downtown government buildings and upscale commercial centers. Government-sponsored high-density housing, both in the form of new construction and limited rehabilitation, was implemented. The planners knew that new buildings necessitated clearing away defunct buildings. Their planning epistemology depended on a rationale, and the convenient syllogism was the disease. A neighborhood whose houses showed evidence of deterioration was a diseased neighborhood. The cure was civic surgery in the hospital of urban renewal, and the doctors were politicians and public agency administrators. On a larger scale, major "surgery, grafting was the planners' pseudo-science to the service of the cultural and economic prejudices of those controlling urban renewal. The city was sick and had to be cured. Using medical metaphors gives the sense of organic phenomena. The city operates well but now and then has some aberrations—some cancers. Cut out the cancers, goes the argument, and the body will continue its proper functioning."[15]

A major urban renewal program was freeway construction through the urban core of American cities. In Minneapolis and St. Paul, highway planners surveyed wide swaths through neighborhoods to be clear-cut and paved in order to connect major roadways with the centers of downtowns. Interdisciplinary teams of engineers, architects, planners and sociologists formulated an American ideal of "creating major engineering works, such as an urban freeway system, that can become beautiful public monuments, enhancing the city in which they were built—a force to reform and revitalize the city."[16] Citizen resistance to the freeways was typically unsuccessful. The result is permanent scars that have caused abrupt demarcations, separating one neighborhood from another.

In the mid-1960s, President Lyndon Johnson's Great Society program made substantial contributions to the fledgling urban renewal process. Perhaps the largest and most long lasting of these was the passage of the 1965 Housing and Urban Development Act. This act established the Department of Housing and Urban Development (HUD), which absorbed certain federal departments such as the Federal Housing Administration and the Farmers Home Administration. It also consolidated ten development programs into a single development block grant program established by the Community Development Assistance Act of 1974. Model cities, water-and-sewer programs and other HUD development programs would reduce paperwork and red tape and expand state and local responsibility for planning and executing development activities.[17]

REACTIONS TO THE DREAM

Don't it always seem to go
That you don't know what you've got till it's gone.
They paved paradise and put up a parking lot.
—Joni Mitchell, "Big Yellow Taxi," 1970

In 1961, Jane Jacobs published her epic critique *The Death and Life of Great American Cities*, which presented a thoughtful reaction to urban renewal. Her book energized the later-to-come organized movements to oppose urban renewal as administered by public agencies.

Perhaps there is no way to list all of the urban renewal critics who have elucidated its failures. Most of them point out its misguided attempts to revive faltering downtowns and its inability to find proper housing for the poor, especially with high-rise public housing. Urban renewal today continues to sponsor sports stadiums isolated from the rest of the city, fortress-like retail centers and concrete sinews of expressways that tear through and destroy neighborhoods.[18] Today, too many of those downtown retail centers (many inappropriately Xerox-copied from their suburban counterparts) now bring blight back downtown, while enough of them have been made over to engender a new architectural style that could be called "Urban Renewal Revival." Most urban planners working today acknowledge these permanent scars in the nation's cityscapes.

By the 1970s, citizen groups in many major cities developed opposition to urban renewal plans affecting their communities. In Boston, community activists halted construction of the proposed Southwest Expressway—but only after a three-mile-long stretch of land had been cleared. In San Francisco, Joseph Alioto was the first mayor to publicly repudiate the policy of urban renewal, and with the backing of community groups, he forced the state to end construction of highways through the heart of the city.

In almost all of these cases, a paramount failure of high-strata public administrators was their lack of recognition that their plans reflecting their professional expertise and their grandiose ambitions flew in the face of what local citizens knew better than anyone else. As noted by architectural critic Witold Rybczynski, its practitioners were "more concerned with what is 'good for people' rather than discovering what people want."[19]

As America began to experience the emerging status of professional citizens, people from various career tracks became aware and concerned about the misfit of public planning in their urban surroundings. They became sufficiently self-educated and volunteered their parallel expertise, able to discern the most workable solution to affect their community's welfare. They could sense the appropriate aesthetics and became aware of public administrators' most critical lack of vision: the livability of community environs. Although this 1960s urban renewal epoch was provident for modern architecture, as large, clear-cut properties became filled with new structures expressing attempts at architectural individualism, this outcome did not become fully embraced by the public at large. The buildings' scale and deliberate avoidance of articulated surfaces seemed impersonal and irrelevant. What eventually came into play was these citizens' intuitive reckoning that rampant modernity should no longer be the default mechanism for emerging enlightened attitudes. They realized the venerable architecture of previous times could no longer be swept into the dustpans of history.

CHAPTER 6

The Minneapolis Housing and Redevelopment Authority (HRA)

As an architect, if I had no economic or social limitations, I'd solve my problems with one-story buildings. Imagine how pleasant it would be to always work and plan in spaces overlooking lovely gardens and flowers. Yet we know that within the framework of our present cities this is impossible to achieve. Why? Because we must recognize social and economic limitations and requirements. A solution without such recognition would be meaningless.
—Minoru Yamasaki, architect (along with George Hellmuth) for the Pruitt–Igoe Public Housing Project in St. Louis

The Minneapolis Housing and Redevelopment Authority (HRA) began its operations in the post–Word War II era with the mission to revitalize various declining areas of Minneapolis at a time when the city was undergoing disinvestment due to both the public and private market force's attention to suburban growth. Many of its top-level staff members were former World War II military officers who translated their military authority to administrating HRA.[20] HRA found demolition as an effective mechanism to eradicate deterioration, and the Minneapolis Gateway area was a testament to that process, as that area of downtown Minneapolis's earliest beginnings in the 1860s became one of the nation's largest area-wide demolition programs a century later in the 1960s. The clear-cut eradication of acres of blighted buildings was immediately seen as a success, and demolition became a useful redevelopment tool whenever HRA thought it necessary.

The General Neighborhood Renewal Plan (GNRP), a federal program of the Federal Home Finance Agency and a precursor to HUD, was a main redevelopment tool. Its practitioners believed in the "neighborhood perfected" model, advocating tearing out substandard properties rather than improving them.

When Bob Jorvig was succeeded by Chuck Krusell, an accountant, HRA took a pragmatic approach to urban development. One of the most important and effective HRA leaders was Dick Brustad, whose early experience came in early neighborhood redevelopment, wherein he employed academic-based approaches. Near North was a major focus for HRA, and Brustad became one of the main planners for that area. After Near North began, Northeast neighborhoods such as Saint Anthony began renewal operations. In these areas, demolition remained a significant redevelopment tool in companionship with suburban-style new-house construction, with remodeling certain existing houses used as an occasional selective tool.[21]

In 1960, the Seward neighborhood became an official renewal area and was broken down into four sections: Seward East, Seward Southeast, Seward West and Seward South. Seward East, where the housing stock needed only basic repairs, became the first renewal area, with isolated demolition and new-house replacement in the form of low-pitched roof ranch houses. Seward West became the next area, but its housing stock was designated for widespread demolition. Chuck Krusell foresaw neighborhood opposition. "People won't put up with it," he said.

The Seward West Renewal Plan was largely based on an academic model, incorporating the "neighborhood perfected" standard, and had limited appreciation for Seward West's worker housing, which is simpler and less attractive than middle-class housing. Worker housing had modest decorative elements and typically more deferred maintenance, thus presenting less enticement for retention and rehab.

The fundamental mechanics of an urban renewal program are based on HUD-provided funding, with local government offering a sizeable amount, typically in the form of infrastructure such as streets, public utilities, parks and schools. The local HRA prepared a program that received back-and-forth coordination and iterative revisions with HUD. Major components of the proposed program were determined by availability of funds for specific purposes. HRA would send the completed proposed program to HUD. Eventually, after various revisions and amendments, HUD approved it in a contract form.

Citizen participation was a "big-time" item, according to many HUD people. (Minneapolis had two big projects at the time: Seward West and West Bank; it was a "busy" time, according to former HUD staff member Patricia Mack.)[22] The previous Seward East program utilized what had become the traditional citizens' advisory committee, which was gratuitously inclined to accept public agency plans for the neighborhood, taking the agency's decisions as coming from the government, whose beneficence placed the public interest foremost in their minds. What's more, if they were to disagree, the bottom line was that the city agency—not the neighborhood—had the experts, and their words were to be obeyed.

At the outset of the Seward West Renewal Program, the Seward West Advisory Committee exercised its role of obedience, but it may have heard voices of older residents who opposed the program. Nonetheless, the advisory committee stayed the course, as it believed government was acting in the best interest of the people. But these older residents, who had lived their working-class lives by that same principle, were now somehow in doubt, combined with fear and resentment. Meanwhile, Seward West resident Jeri Reilly and other neighborhood residents began to realize that the Seward West Advisory Committee representatives did not question authority, which put them at odds with both the traditional residents and the emerging activists, who were making up a significant segment of the neighborhood. The activists began to plan to remove the advisory group. This nascent resistance, however, was unknown to those in public agencies and to many people living in Seward West.

ORGANIZED OPPOSITION TO DEMOLITION BEGINS: THE AD HOC COMMITTEE TO REBUILD SEWARD WEST

Don't stop, thinking about tomorrow.
Don't stop, it'll soon be here.
It'll be better than before.
Yesterday's gone, yesterday's gone.
Fleetwood Mac, "Don't Stop," 1977

In August 1970, Don Barton came to Minneapolis from Columbus, Ohio, after VISTA training in Chicago. VISTA (Volunteers in Service to America) was a federal service originally envisioned by President John F. Kennedy and founded in 1965. It was intended to be the domestic version of the Peace Corps. A local activist organization assigned Don to work as a community organizer in local housing issues. His first housing-related assignment was to look for a place to live, so as he came down Franklin Avenue and then happened to look south down Milwaukee Avenue, he exclaimed, "Oh my God, let me get out of there!" Soon after, Don found a duplex unit to rent on nearby Twenty-second Avenue, and his next look at Milwaukee Avenue made him think, "This is an interesting street." Later, Don noted that he "got to know the people who lived there, and then I could relate the people with the houses they lived in…how it was part of their lives, as if they had lived there forever."[23]

At the September 1970 public hearing on Seward West at Matthews Center, Don was surprised when "most of the public grumbled and expressed opposition to the Seward West renewal plan…but HRA wanted to install a program nobody wanted." He soon discovered that the representative neighborhood group—the Seward West Advisory Committee—was basically agreeable to HRA policy. Later, Don found a neighborhood group opposed to the renewal plan and began to apply his VISTA skills to help organize the group into the Ad Hoc Committee to Rebuild Seward West. A six-member steering committee of four homeowners and two tenants represented a cross section of the neighborhood. Don thought an important aspect of the group would be having a mix of both young and old, and he soon found and recruited Gladys Cowan and Rose Hendron. These two women had lived on the same block on Twenty-third Avenue all their lives, now accompanied by their children and grandchildren, who lived down the block and across the street.

The ad hoc committee's purpose was to form a renewal plan that would "save houses in repairable condition and replace substandard housing with low- and moderate-income family homes, consisting of owner-occupied, cooperative and rental units."[24] The group secured the support of the Committee on Social Action of the Minnesota Synod Lutheran Church in America, a coalition of mostly young secular people committed to striving for social change.

In November 1971, the committee circulated a petition for appeal of the Seward West Renewal Project. A meeting at Matthews Center attended by approximately forty people began the first step in the group's campaign, which set in motion more vigorous opposition to the renewal plan. The committee demanded the "immediate review of any and all plans affecting the neighborhood and the assistance and full cooperation of all public and private agencies and groups in any way involved with the Seward West Renewal Project."

Appendix II of the committee's petition to appeal the existing renewal plan report described a survey undertaken by the committee that included both interior and exterior inspections of eighteen houses in HRA's "To Be Acquired" list (designated for demolition), eleven of them for substandard and deteriorated conditions and seven for "planning reasons," meaning the houses that were located on lots too narrow for conventional zoning or with insufficient side yards.

The inspection report in Appendix II noted that the "substandard and deteriorated" classification by HRA was an inadequate measure of the homes, "especially in light of the fact that many people have recently been letting their homes deteriorate, not knowing when and if their homes are to be taken." No more homes should be acquired, the report stated, until a more thorough survey is taken by HRA, and dwellings found to be structurally sound or capable of rehabilitation would be removed from the acquisition list.

Following are typical entries found in the inspection portion of the report:

> *Picture IV: 2308 Milwaukee Av. S. This is a duplex with 1 bedroom per unit. The owner-occupant is Mr. Robert C. Hurd, who has kept the house up to code and recently added a bathroom and bedroom in the basement. The interior is in excellent condition, and the same is true of the exterior. The owners definitely want to stay.*

> *Picture VI: 2214 24th Av. S. This is a 3-bedroom home and is owned by the occupant, Mrs. Silverstein. She is a widow and lets out three rooms to supplement her income. She feels the house is completely adequate and has kept it up to code. She is planning to paint the living room when she is able to afford it. She is determined to keep her house. She feels that she and her husband worked too hard to buy the home and maintain it in good condition to let it go. She is convinced that there is nothing comparable to it that she could buy. She does not want to live in a senior citizens' high-rise.*

> *Picture VII: 2103 23rd Av. S. Mr. and Mrs. J. Adkinson are the owner-occupants of this 1-bedroom home. They have lived here for 21 years. The condition of the interior and exterior of this building could not be improved upon. Among the recent improvements are: new furnace, new roof, new siding. The owners definitely want to remain in their home.*

Notes: The above address listed as 2214 24th Av. S is probably one of two houses existing today, side by side, either 2212 or 2216 24th Avenue South. 2103 23rd Avenue South remains—in fine condition—across Twenty-third Avenue from the Milwaukee Avenue Four-Block Area. Its single-bedroom status has been increased with a rear addition, which nicely complements the house's more notable status. It is listed on the National Register of Historic Places as an individual designation.

Of the eleven houses listed in the committee's inspection report, seven remain today: 2308 Milwaukee Avenue, 2201–03 Twenty-second Avenue South, 2103 Twenty-third Avenue South, 2301 Twenty-third Avenue South, 2313 East Twenty-fourth Street, 2412 Twenty-fourth Avenue South and 2412 Twenty-fourth Avenue South.

At this time, the ad hoc committee had an active but unofficial role in representing citizens of this urban renewal area. Nonetheless, HRA and the city council recognized the Seward West Advisory Committee as the designated neighborhood citizen organization, in accordance with how neighborhood renewal programs had typically been administered. This committee's passive role to HRA formulated no initiatives or planning ideas put on the table by them. By mid-1971, this traditional citizens' group had been upended by the emergence of a group calling itself a project area committee, decidedly more active and eager to challenge authority and "feeling that the time for advice was past and the time for control of our own destiny was here now."

Winds of change were coming, but no storm warnings had been issued.

On November 2, 1971, Larry Fortmann, president of the newly reconstituted project area committee, wrote a letter to the HRA executive director stating, "We have a fondness for old picturesque houses—Milwaukee Avenue runs through our heart."[25]

The HRA plan proposing clearance of approximately 70 percent of the houses in Seward West, or almost four hundred homes, precipitated strong reactions in the neighborhood. The ad hoc committee examined the HRA plan in its general context and then developed a detailed examination and supporting documentation. At the conclusion of the ad hoc committee work, PAC adopted the following policy statement:

Preserve and rehabilitate as much as humanly possible the existing homes in Seward West.
Replace those that can't be preserved with buildings of similar size and price.

Allow anyone who wants to stay in Seward West to do so.
Allow owner-occupants to stay in their homes if they so desire.

If the advisory committee had remained unchallenged, the landscape and people living in Seward West would be vastly different. One dramatic difference would have been the obliteration of Milwaukee Avenue. The traditional advisory committee seemed to have a Velveeta cheese and saltine cracker sensibility, while PAC developed an appetite for food fights. PAC committed itself to carrying out the principles of its policy statement, accomplished by its grab of control and imagination. Over a short period of time, the ad hoc committee had done the set-up work for PAC and had disbanded.

CHAPTER 7

The Seward West Project Area Committee (PAC)

The Seward West Project Area Committee (PAC) was composed of twenty-two volunteer members who were residents living within the Seward West neighborhood or who had businesses in the neighborhood. PAC's leadership consisted of a president, vice-president, secretary and treasurer. PAC's official meetings were held every other Thursday evening in Matthews Center. PAC's official function, as mandated by HUD, was to act as a liaison between the Minneapolis Housing and Redevelopment Authority, which was administrating renewal activities, and the residents of the Seward West neighborhood. In actuality, however, after the neighborhood's rejection of the advisory committee status, PAC developed a very aggressive stance and nuanced political connections. Eventually, PAC gained an active role in making decisions on issues both large and small. PAC's tactics, so intense in the spirit of those days of confrontation, with activists railing against authority, challenged HRA at every opportunity in ways that kept the agency on the defensive. Eventually, this strategy became a major factor in the committee's success.

THE SEWARD WEST PAC'S POLITICAL BASIS

PAC members' leftist or liberal convictions were as much cultural as political. Prior generations of college-age young people shared their parents' attitudes on anti-communism, but many in this generation likely had read Marx and socialist thinkers as a means of comparative knowledge without rejecting ideas of capitalism as a default system worth working for them. Many PAC members had merged their leftist beliefs with a form of populism. (This nation has a long-standing recurrent "populist" tradition, which historically serves both progressive and reactionary causes.) Many of their ideas might have been influenced by older neighborhood residents, who provided a close-up perspective of the local situation. This synchronized with their new leftism and commitment to social causes.

The New American Movement (NAM) was organized in 1971 by radical political activists seeking to create a successor organization to Students for a Democratic Society (SDS), once a leading extremist organization of the New Left movement in America. Similar to the Seward West PAC, the founding activists behind NAM were vigorous opponents of the war in Vietnam. However, unlike PAC, NAM shared much of its political framework with the New Communist Movement, which was built around local groups emphasizing Marxist study, discussion of contemporary issues, support of local labor actions and work in the community to raise awareness. Several NAM members lived in Seward West. NAM members occasionally engaged in informal discussions with PAC members and eagerly offered to assist PAC with its activities. However, NAM's overt political framework didn't fit with PAC's main objective of HRA combat but with avoidance of extreme political groups.

NAM rented a former church building on Franklin Avenue for a few years. When it moved out, PAC moved into the building for its office. For some strange reason, the mailman continued to deliver NAM's mail to the PAC office for several years despite PAC's informing the post office otherwise. PAC wanted no association with the now-defunct extreme fringe organization; however, for the PAC staff, reading NAM's mail proved amusing.

Similarly, PAC did not operate with anarchic behavior, unlike many of the food co-ops that formed the undergirding of counterculture at that time. With the typical food co-op, nobody was really in charge, but PAC's leadership, both formal and informal, was readily apparent.

PAC's political influences rose out of the Minneapolis Democratic-Farmer-Labor Party (DFL). Many young DFL members gave much background support to PAC, and one of their own, Tony Scallon, became PAC's dominant leader. But PAC clearly developed its own political model, based more on counterculture activism than the framework of a conventional political party.

Organized meetings and spontaneously occurring discussions helped form PAC's urban renewal decision-making. Then there were the frequent Saturday night parties, attended almost entirely by PAC members and their fringe adherents. Social cohesion was necessary, as most of these people unintentionally abandoned their pre-PAC friendships for this alternative reality.

In the early 1970s, local activists, including many hippies, began to create co-op grocery stores as a logical response to the demand of young radicals for goods and services necessary for living a life outside the established economic system. Craig Cox's perceptive book *Storefront Revolution* notes, "During this time, an alternative economic system created a network of many home-grown enterprises in Minneapolis and St. Paul that allowed countercultural people to buy food at a neighborhood cooperative, live in a tenant-owned housing co-op or informal commune, and earn a living at a worker-owned or worker-managed business. Their kids could attend a cooperative-run daycare center and receive healthcare from a community health clinic paid on a sliding scale. A few cooperative restaurants served 'whole foods.' Also, co-ops organized workshops of current issues, and cultural events were organized."[26] Many of these co-ops are operating today, expanding in scope and attracting middle-class customers beyond their original sub-neighborhood bases.

Nonetheless, Marxist dogma, one of the cooperative movement's influences, played no real role in PAC thinking. Although PAC operated in the flow of the counterculture very active on the West Bank at that time, it held no protest rallies or demonstrations. "Charlie don't surf" was a famous line from the 1979 film *Apocalypse Now*, and PAC didn't march.

Tony Scallon Enters the Room

Many PAC members were students and ex-students who had "come of age" a generation later than those college students who pursued history or political science as a continuum of traditional academics. Their studies of humanities and liberal arts propelled these young people to see a need for societal and cultural change. Hippies believed utopias were within their reach. For example, two communes located in Seward West were attempts at being localized embodiments of homegrown utopias.

Tony Scallon, a parochial school teacher, became part of PAC's formation in 1971, forging a coalition of young college-age people recently arrived to the area, longtime and elderly residents and one conservative middle-age businessman. Tony's political objective intended to provide the balance that could not only achieve realistic policies but also send a message to public agency doubters that the PAC was not simply a band of young crazies. This was a much-needed identity in an era known for its assortment of particular young people occasionally called "misguided youth" at best and "dangerous" at other times.

PAC's modus operandi consisted of leadership and decision-making by the younger set, supported by older members who had lived in the neighborhood all their lives. These longtime residents gave occasional strongly voiced support and active participation, rendering a sense of legitimacy to the organization.

Tony also worked with a handful of "Young Turks," who brought about a wave of change within the local Democratic-Farmer-Labor Party. These people lived in various parts of nearby neighborhoods and thus were not eligible to become official PAC members, but they were regular attendees at PAC meetings. These sessions were typically followed by a few hours at a bar on Franklin Avenue or, sometimes, on the West Bank, an area whose activists were likewise immersed in their vigorous (and ultimately successful) opposition to the renewal plan underway in that area. Although PAC meetings carried out official business formulated by its twenty-two members, the after-meeting bar sessions often created the overall strategy (some said the real PAC business happened here) out of the fecund ideas of young minds fresh out of college. They were now engaging in a new reality that these times and the zeitgeist in the air invited us to change. Here in the early 1970s, certain cultural forces, immeasurable but somehow tangible at the time, were about to change everything around us. Somehow, we seemed swept into place.

Many of the young activists in the meeting audiences became regular attendees and eventually were drawn into the discussions that were forming directives and policies. The bar scenes always instigated quick back-and-forth discussions in which they could more easily give voice to the matters at hand. Tony's political instincts, always at heightened alert, could sense which of those people could become good PAC members. He would begin his recruiting by vigorously arguing with them and then drawing their thinking into PAC mode. In this way, the audience at PAC meetings became something like a farm team, where Tony could recruit appropriate new members.

At this time, no one in the group had heard of Jane Jacobs, but their thinking on the matters at hand in Seward West came right out of her book, *The Death and Life of Great American Cities.* Jacobs was known to engage in causes without ideology, as did PAC. Observers of Jacobs considered her writing "intensely suspicious of centralized planning" in various terms—neo-conservative or libertarian.[27] Harvard social scientist Nathan Glazer somewhat agreed on the anarchistic description, commenting that her thinking that "people making their own decisions, with less or no guidance or control from above, will make a better city."[28] It may be accurate to say that PAC belonged to no single socio-political label, but a rough guide in that direction might indicate the group to be an amalgam of a very populist liberalism and pragmatic anarchism.

At PAC meetings, not making quorum was unthinkable—most if not all members were nearly always present, sitting at a long table. The audience sitting on folding chairs against the four walls of the meeting room consisted of several HRA staff members and curious longtime neighborhood residents and political activists from outside the neighborhood who were attracted to the scene like moths to an electric light. New upstart progressive and radical groups with allied interests occasionally came out of a sense of solidarity with PAC's purpose. One memorable group was the Solid Oak Carpentry Collective, which dedicated itself to establishing a volunteer base of young activists and older retired carpenters who would rebuild the older bedraggled houses in the neighborhood. The young activists, appearing in mild hippie mode, spoke earnestly about formulating a philosophy to define their mission; the older carpenters stated that they were anxious to get their tools to work.

In PAC's early days, several neighborhood residents formed an intense core of activists who threw themselves into PAC's efforts. Their work became indivisible from that of PAC members and staff and formed highly influential contributions that had highly critical outcomes.

New PAC members were occasionally needed. Often a new member sprang forth with new ideas and the energy needed to meet PAC's evolving state of operation. They replaced those who now seemed out of step, those who were once a bright new star but who no longer fit the evolving process that fine-tuned PAC's thinking. Ever-changing challenges were always coming at the organization. Continuing to be a PAC member required a resilience and stamina with which an always-contentious group had to operate. In hindsight, it is difficult to estimate the average period of membership within PAC's ten-year existence. Some served a bit more than a year, others continued for several years and only a few remained for PAC's entire ten-year duration.

Likewise, PAC leadership recycled during PAC's existence. Tony dominated the president's chair through most of its years, while subcommittee leaders typically served a few years at a time. Most important is the fact that PAC's principal leaders—Tony Scallon, Don Barton, Steve Swanson, Kathy Johnson and others—were active from its beginning until the 1980s, when the renewal program reached completion.

Rudi Anders came to Seward West in 1971 in pursuit of a PhD in political history at the University of Minnesota. As a self-described academic leftist, Anders joined the PAC, recruited by Tony. Rudi noted of his first PAC meeting:

> *What struck me is that these folks did not see these problems in terms of a larger framework—nothing other than that the architects or planners or developers were the enemy. Clearly, most of us shared the notion that we were dealing with a downtown elite of developers, developer-friendly planners and politicians who wanted to destroy a neighborhood of single- or multi-family homes into a sea for low-rise apartments to serve the needs of the university and the hospitals. In fact, the emphasis on single-family ownership and the "village" of Seward West amazed me—it was the small-town vision, the place where we all knew each other. When viewed in the larger perspective, one had to admit that the planners and developers were only doing what seemed to be the natural progression in all American cities—the continued destruction of neighborhoods to expand the core city. This meant that they wanted higher density and assumed, as so many "social scientists" at the time assumed, that they had the answer to creating the perfect future city.* [29]

Rudi and several others saw PAC as an "odd combination of limited-government lefties, or liberals operating in the sense that they might have had a more communitarian philosophy and abandonment of 'traditional' values as related to sexual, social and work standards of the time."

Early PAC activity attracted several people on the far left as well as a few on the far right—both paradoxically espousing similar objectives of mistrust of government and anti-renewal attitudes. But the brain trust of PAC, led by Tony Scallon, purged extremists and developed a moderate-to-liberal coalition based much more on pragmatism than political ideology. [30]

Oddly enough, it was after PAC had purged the extremists that the "basic disagreements" began a long period of infighting within PAC, resulting in two core groups. Each side sought to continue PAC's fundamental mission to prevent the neighborhood from succumbing to planners and developers patterning the natural progression in all American cities: the continued destruction of neighborhoods to expand the core city. Although adhering to the principles of Jane Jacobs, each group held to differing methods to prevent this from happening in Seward West, one by waging battles of confrontation against authority and planning and the other by substituting its own alternate planning. Each group opposed the other's actions with various strategies of power contests that, at various times, attempted to induce non-aligned PAC members to join their side, doing so in ways that stayed off the table at PAC meetings—until it came time to vote on certain resolutions.

The infighting certainly frayed many nerves, spoiled friendships and generally made working together on overall goals more difficult. But with the Seward West PAC, these scrimmages provided a certain value as they made people more productive by providing creative tension and also steered the organization away from the groupthink that eventually stultified other community organizations.

CHAPTER 8

The Seward West Renewal Plan

THE MINNEAPOLIS HOUSING AND REDEVELOPMENT AUTHORITY AND SEWARD WEST

HRA's South Area Office, located at the edge of Seward West, functioned as the administrative center for its Seward West operations. The staff director was Jack Crimmins, a World War II military veteran. His dapper suits and tightly patterned neckties suggested a somewhat bureaucratic formality. He was tall, balding and had a pencil-thin mustache, rendering a dominant presence that was useful for his objectives to treat neighborhood activists with a suave superiority and indirect disdain.

By the early 1970s, public agency administrators were coming from civilian backgrounds, somewhat diluting but not substantially replacing the top-down authoritative structure. In an era in which the newly formed HUD had begun to promulgate measures that recognized citizen participation, Crimmins's military bearing cemented his dedication to the traditional model of the profession of public planning. These professional planners kept largely apart from political forces to the extent possible, taking it for granted that they should perform their work without heeding the advice or direction of the citizenry they told themselves they were dedicated to serve. To put it more bluntly, many of them held distaste for citizen participation. These administrators set themselves into static modes of action and thinking, ironically evading the future, which is planning's purpose. Instead, these planners seemed unaware that cultural change was undergoing the most dramatic transformation in the history of cities during the 1970s.[31]

The Crimmins-led office formed a formidable opponent for the PAC, which knew it was operating in a milieu that required oppositional tactics in the form of confrontation tinged with well-articulated anger and, above all, well-prepared presentations. With key PAC leaders Tony Scallon, Steve Swanson and Kathy Johnson's adept verbal jousting, PAC staff gradually developed the ability to out-duel HRA's minions.

In the summer months, Tony set aside his teaching responsibilities to join PAC staff members, Legal Aid attorney Steve Swanson and freelance legal pugilist Jack Cann in afternoon meetings at HRA's downtown headquarters. In this setting, Jack Crimmins and his supporting cast of upper-echelon administrators could bring out their large maps, thick planning manuals and a long conference table lined with bureaucratic experts of various segments of public policy. Their effort intended to bring down the weight of professionalism on the less experienced PAC representatives. In this setting, Crimmins seemed to operate from a position of strength. But PAC had the urban guerrilla advantage—it owned the night. When meetings were held in the evenings at Matthews Center, PAC could hang on definitions of a single word or extend discussion of its contentions into finer and still finer points, often dragging out meetings for hours, while the HRA people became inwardly exasperated about missing their favorite TV shows in the comfort of their homes.

PAC's highly argumentative extenuation of every issue put on the table created an invariably long, boring and dreary process. It certainly consumed long periods of time. But the adrenalin-fueled PAC knew of the possible but oftentimes seemingly unlikely payoff. What HRA staff negotiators thought they had going for themselves was their policy-shaped logic, which would be important and necessary if they wanted to prevail. But PAC's counterattack was to make its statements in an "I dare you" manner.

HRA Perfidy Reaches Melodramatic Proportions

Jack Crimmins's downfall, in Don Barton's words, was the fact that "his physical appearance and his righteousness made him a potent target for PAC to rally against." Sometime during the midpoint of the PAC-HRA battle, Don, Jeri and a few other PAC people realized that their frequent sarcastic humor that surfaced in describing the absurdities of this political clash could lead to the next step—staging a melodrama complete with a full cast of characters. It would be called *The Seward West Side Story*. Jeri played Miss Sally Sweetheart, a young innocent unaware that the HRA had misled her neighborhood about its nefarious plans to obliterate it. Don played Roger Rehab, the hero who eventually rescued everyone and everything. Marlys Thoreen wore a slinky silver lamé dress and played a temptress who promised bureaucratic benefits. But the pièce de résistance was Don's roommate, Mike Cain, who wore a rubber bald pate, trimmed his mustache to pencil-thin proportions, dressed like a loan shark and played the part of Criminal C. Crimmins—no attempt here to politely disguise the villain's identity.[32]

The high point of the melodrama came when Criminal C. visited Miss Gladys Goodheart, a kind elderly lady, and threatened to force her out of her house and into the cold. Miss Goodheart was played by Gladys Cowan, also thinly disguised, wearing her typical grandmother-like dress and shawl, curly gray hair and wire-rimmed glasses. In real life, her house was threatened with HRA demolition. As Criminal C. sneered so dramatically, with Mike exhibiting Jack's public meeting mannerisms, the full-house crowd hissed and booed and then cheered profusely when Roger Rehab appeared at the last minute, donning white long johns and a red cape, to save Gladys, Miss Sally and Seward West.

Longtime PAC member Kent Robbins, who eventually became a Minneapolis City Council policy coordinator, gives the Crimmins scenario considerable insight. "Even though HUD had introduced citizen participation in renewal programs," he said, "Jack believed in the old-style authority model. Meanwhile, Tony was smart enough to realize, unlike so many Southside Minneapolis grass-roots politicians who believed issues were more important than loyalty, that the Northside political machine, honed on generations of interfamily loyalty, held the real power—in the city council and HRA. Tony gained the trust of the ultimate Northsider, future mayor Al Hofstede, who soon dominated the city power base. Al knew Tony's energy."[33]

Kent noted that Crimmins saw PAC's raw intelligence, but he couldn't outlast them in the long run. Why? Cheap rent—that was the basis for so many Seward West people staying and not moving, even the renters. Jack probably thought that they would go away after finishing college. But when they finished grad school or got entry-level jobs, many stayed in the neighborhood.

"Jack also could not outlast the post-LBJ urban renewal HUD-mandated citizen participation models that set up PACs," added Robbins. "So Jack became worn down. His Northside powerbase had seen Tony and Southside politicos secure the allegiance of the liberal state legislature. Jack had relied on his military background of operating from the status quo, but the Northside politicians moved beyond him."[34]

In 1974, HRA's downtown office pulled Crimmins out of his directorship of the South Area Office. Assistant Director Bob Scroggins took his position. Scroggins and fellow staffer Bill Schatzlein saw the Seward West urban renewal program as a system of policies that needed objective analysis and the means to resolve issues and basic HRA objectives by accommodating all parties involved. The Crimmins war mentality was out of the picture. The HRA South Area Office welcomed PAC to share some administrative responsibilities. Meanwhile, HRA held to the basic tenets of its demolition-oriented renewal plan while offering a reasoned approach to engage PAC in various deliberations.

NEWSPAPER COLUMNIST BARBARA FLANAGAN WALKS DOWN MILWAUKEE AVENUE

In mid-April 1972, after many autumn afternoons walking down Milwaukee Avenue, I photographed what seemed to be a romantic setting of decrepitude. I took eight of my photographs to the *Minneapolis Star Tribune*'s reception area, along with a note addressed to Barbara Flanagan, whose columns on architecture were beginning to develop public interest in historic preservation. I added my work phone number and mentioned that I would be glad to accompany her on a tour of Milwaukee Avenue. While I was driving back to work, I wondered how I'd get those photos back after what I expected to be a non-response.

The following afternoon, Barbara called, expressing all of her trademark enthusiasm, and took my offer for a tour and set a date.

Walking down the street, Barbara proved to be a delightful commentator and stopped to talk to a few residents. One longtime homeowner, Agnes Lund, chatted about having lived sixteen years in her house, which Barbara described as "cozy, clean and comfortable," with no major rehabilitation done for twelve years because of the urban renewal question.

A week later, Barbara's April 18, 1972 article expressed an optimism ornamented by her phrases as she extolled praise of what the street offered. She concluded her article by stating that many people have learned to appreciate some of the values of city neighborhoods that our parents once had but became rejected a generation before us. "We sit on our porches," she wrote. "We walk to the park, the store, to church and to work. We think ours is a lifestyle worth rediscovering and preserving. To do that, we must preserve the homes people live in. And to do that, we've got to convince the urban renewal people that it can be done."

The effects of her column could be measured in four ways: it created a sizable positive reaction among the public that typically followed her columns, it gave PAC a certain public credibility and confidence that it otherwise would not have received in those early days of the struggle, it put HRA on notice and proved that PAC was not the immature group of young idealists it wanted them to appear to be and, most importantly, it gave Milwaukee Avenue status as a legitimate and endangered historic preservation issue.

The Barbara Flanagan article continued to bolster PAC's publicity campaign. In a moment of boldness, PAC decided to reach for bigger media stakes—the *Star Tribune*'s *Picture* magazine, which appeared in each Sunday edition of the paper. Various PAC members crafted a PR document to send to the newspaper. In short order, *Tribune* writer Howard Erickson and noted photographer Richard Olsenius called, and PAC members happily fed them what they thought these young journalists wanted to hear.

Early on the morning of Sunday, November 19, 1972, the cover of the *Star Tribune*'s *Picture* magazine was emblazoned with a striking, large and boldly colorful photograph of 2117 Milwaukee Avenue's sagging front porch, above which read the headline: "Milwaukee Avenue—Worth Saving?" Richard Olsenius's "new realism" photographs comfortably rendered the poignancy of the time at hand and the faded presence of a glory to be reclaimed. But in the words of staff writer Howard Erickson, outright cynicism pervaded his portrayal of PAC and its cause. The first sentence set the tone: "Milwaukee Av. S. has some of the sorriest-looking, most decrepit decaying houses in Minneapolis, crammed together on crumbling foundations without basements." The phones began ringing at the homes of various PAC members. A collective paranoia, a condition often endemic to counterculture authority-resisting groups, was setting in. PAC had been slammed.

Tony called an emergency afternoon meeting at the PAC office and dictated to each person what to write. From all of us present, expletives, many with Erickson's name attached, flew through the air. People in the room felt we had been dealt a serious setback that HRA would use against us.

Later that day, several of Tony's friends called him with congratulations. Soon after, the cognoscenti of various counterculture publications, flourishing in 1970s-era Minneapolis, praised what they saw as a cynical press in league with various powers-that-be, which PAC stood up to with conviction and conscience. Somehow, Erickson's derisive description of PAC members as "idealists" read as a positive portrayal. Olsenius's sixteen well-composed photographs, placed throughout the eleven-page article, augmented this idealism by revealing a promise that could be sensed beyond the decrepitude.

The following Sunday, November 26, 1972, the *Tribune*'s editorial page was headlined "Milwaukee Ave: They Say Yes, It's Worth Saving." The article was replete with supportive letters boosting the PAC's cause with insights beyond its close-up focus. Frank Kratky commented, "The wholesale removal of all existing deteriorated buildings isn't the answer because it will simultaneously uproot, displace and ultimately destroy the neighborhood character and its continuity with the past." Another contributor stated, "Progress and urban renewal, hand in glove with bankers, contractors and speculators, have consistently lowered the quality and raised the cost of living." In no way outdone, Tony's letter claimed that Erickson's article "not only exhibits blatant editorializing uncalled for in responsible journalism but also contains gross misrepresentations of several important facts." Other letters to the editor opposing demolition and supporting preservation followed in later issues. Those letters gained PAC long-lasting traction, credibility and a different collective supportive consciousness.

CHAPTER 9
PAC Planning Begins

Come on now people
Let's get on the ball
And work together
Come on, come on
Let's work together
Canned Heat, "Let's Work Together," 1970

One cold winter evening in 1972, several PAC members gathered in PAC activist Don Barton's duplex unit on Twenty-third Avenue. The purpose of the gathering was to form what would become the New Plan and Structures Subcommittee (NPS), a planning subcommittee within PAC. People sat in well-worn chairs around a dining room table of thrift store origin, most of them of a younger age group. But Gladys Cowan, one of two senior citizens in the room, sat in a rocking chair with her nimble fingers working darning needles and yarn, looking like a Norman Rockwell painting—except for the space heater, with its black sheet-metal chimney, in the background. Her neighbor Rose Hendron sat quietly at the table.

NPS would complement PAC's political action with its own urban design planning process and begin the neighborhood's earliest efforts to effect physical change to keep the traditional character of Seward West. This meant departing from the abstractions of political policy to examine the rehabilitation potential of the houses and their environs. This view differed significantly from that of HRA, which envisioned an area drastically rebuilt with new apartment buildings and rambler-style houses, similar to what it had produced in earlier renewal plans in Northeast and Northside Minneapolis.

As land-use issues became tied to rehab, NPS gained more committee members, and its twice-monthly meetings became open to the general PAC membership and the public.

At this very time, several neighborhoods in Minneapolis were being outfitted with modern architecture. The need for affordable housing was being met by cities' emerging commitment to provide affordable housing and by various HUD programs. These financing programs gave opportunity for modern architectural design, as the prevailing assumption was that new construction was the obvious method. Contemporary apartment buildings were constructed on cleared land in the Bethune neighborhood in North Minneapolis, new town houses were built on various sites in Westside St. Paul and clusters of new town houses in the nearby Little Earth housing development filled a large open property near Cedar Avenue and East Twenty-fourth Street. Those town houses were of identical architectural design, set into strips of land intersected by asphalt parking lots. Up Cedar Avenue in the West Bank area, dense high-rise complexes designed by the dean of the University of Minnesota School of Architecture, Ralph Rapson, were in the final design phase, planned for ten stages, and already garnering praise in architecture magazines and occasional supportive articles in the *Minneapolis Star Tribune*. What the newspaper was not reporting, however, was that the neighborhood's project area committee was organizing public resistance, which eventually stopped the development after the first phase was complete.

DRAWING POLITICAL LINES

By this time, PAC's initial objectives were based on the opposition to demolition of most of the neighborhood's houses, requiring the relocation of so many residents that it would eradicate a community in which these people had lived all their lives and cause untenable disruption. As PAC members continued their struggle, they sharpened their rhetoric and combative methods, holding sometimes-weekly meetings that HRA members felt obliged—probably required by their HUD contract—to attend and defend their positions. HRA believed it held all the cards and could rebuff PAC at will. For HRA, this was not the way citizen participation, still a new concept in urban renewal programs, was supposed to function.

As PAC continued its campaign, its leaders decided that the political process to throw out critical HRA renewal program policies needed more than words on paper. Physical planning on paper was needed, too, delineating how properties could be evaluated by an area-wide site plan of PAC's own format, not the HRA land disposition maps. An important byproduct would be urban design documents intended to inform HRA that PAC was capable of more than arguments seemingly intended solely to protest and destroy HRA's program and that the group aimed to redirect the renewal process with a plan more appropriate to the neighborhood.

In early 1973, I joined the PAC staff as a planner. My work was in developing planning documents and site plans that would retain the traditional neighborhood feel in particular areas. On my first day on the job, I received a letter from Larry Irwin, the august and highly esteemed assistant city coordinator and director of the Minneapolis Planning Department, that read as follows: "The staff of the Minneapolis Heritage Preservation Commission has considered the question of the future of the Milwaukee Avenue area. In our opinion, the area, although unique in its own right, does not merit heritage preservation designation. There is an absence of studies demonstrating architectural or historical significance, and the area, in our opinion, does not meet Heritage Preservation Commission criteria."

The letter came in response to my inquiry directed to a planning department staff member who was known to have some expertise in historic preservation, a rare commodity in public agencies at that time. The reply was disappointing but not unexpected. The letter was torn into pieces and then tossed into a wastebasket.

HRA's Seward West area map depicted a property-by-property disposition. Houses were identified by three categories: definite acquisition, conditional acquisition and not to be acquired. Over 70 percent of the houses were listed for definite acquisition, which, within the language of the four-inch-thick HRA renewal document, meant their demolition. The result would be that hundreds of residents would have to leave their houses and the neighborhood they had known all of their lives. Also important was that large areas of the neighborhood were subject to clear-cut physical erasure, and the traditional character of the neighborhood would vanish.

While "deteriorated condition" was the primary reason for demolition, "planning reasons" was a secondary condition. Many houses were built on "substandard-sized" lots with "insufficient side-yards." HRA's technical staff and housing specialists had conducted visual examinations of the exteriors (as well as some interiors) of all the houses in Seward West. In most instances, their exterior condition was evidence enough to warrant demolition: worn-out roofing and siding and other damaged parts. With some houses, structural condition, which typically could be examined only with interior analysis, was the cause for designation. HRA housing specialists estimated whether the cost of rehab would exceed the cost of new replacement. With most dwellings, rehab was judged to be infeasible.

Building code requirements were the basis for their scope of rehabilitation. However, HRA's evaluations also included "modern standards," such as bedroom sizes with sufficient closets, kitchens with up-to-date appliances and cabinets and other appurtenances that the postwar standard of living called for—and which these houses lacked.

These specialists were aware that many Seward West houses had certain elements that no longer met building code requirements that were rarely enforced: pull-chain lighting switches, thirty-amp electrical service and lack of grounded electrical receptacles, unvented plumbing systems, kitchens with wall-mounted sinks and short sections of metal countertops, bathrooms that were entered through kitchens, bathrooms with claw-foot tubs and pull-chain toilets and space heaters in lieu of central heating. Beyond code issues, nicked and pockmarked wide wood trim and other turn-of-the-century millwork made these houses "old-fashioned" in the minds of HRA specialists. Moreover, they felt it their duty to take account of other aspects of updated living environments such as carpet floor coverings, which would be soft on the feet, rather than hardwood; interchangeable storm/screen windows; and that desired goal of so many Americans: one-story houses.

This partial view of a boarded-up house at 2117 Milwaukee Avenue offers a poignant glimpse of degradation that hints at future promise.

These HRA housing specialists were basically reflecting the housing market at the time, which saw its future in the construction of new one-story houses. Extensive house rehabilitation was in no way part of the housing industry, except for remodeling as a means of maintenance, things like shingle replacement, painting and taking out a pair of living-room windows to install a picture window. Rehabilitation was typically dismissed with the following phrase: "Fixing up this old place would cost more than tearing it down and building something new." Contractors knew the uncertainties of new construction were minimal, whereas older buildings had many unknowns, likely resulting from lack of experience in ascertaining the underlying issues an older building might have.

PAC members, however, while agreeing on safety aspects of building codes, found these older houses not outdated and old fashioned but comfortable and charming. Ironically, the criteria HRA used to condemn Seward West houses was the same reason PAC wanted to save them. Worn surfaces had "character" (perhaps being the correct environment in which to wear their noticeably worn denim clothing). In an era in which political humor was nourished with cynicism, PAC members called HRA's plan a "suburbanization" of their neighborhood.

THE BATTLE OF FEW WORDS

The heart of HRA's operating principles was that what was written in its urban renewal plan was, as the expression goes, "written in stone"; it was infallible and could not be changed. Within this heavy book was a sentence stating that all properties in their definite acquisition category "shall be acquired and demolished." The core of PAC's attack aimed at changing this wording to "shall be acquired and *rehabilitated or* demolished." These two words—"rehabilitated" and "or"—became the crux of an intense PAC-HRA battle, with the stakes very high for both sides. Both sides stubbornly held to their positions. PAC legal advisor Steve Swanson, an attorney for the Legal Aid Society, tenaciously articulated PAC's argument while expressing that those two words were reasonable additions and would not contradict HRA's renewal policies. The HRA, however, argued that the word "rehabilitate" in no way belonged in that statement. Both sides could find other aspects of policy to argue about, but the two-word debate remained the main issue. In a large way, the two-word battle affected everything else.

Strong personalities dominated negotiators on both sides. Discussions were exercises in civil intolerance. Finding a middle ground on any issue was not sought as a reasonable means to finding solutions. Neither side was ready to give an inch.

Rudi Anders took occasional breaks in his graduate studies in political history at the University of Minnesota to attend afternoon meetings at the South Area Office or at HRA's downtown main office. Aware he was seeing political history in formation, Rudi could provide scholarly input to his observations of neighborhood issues being argued at the long table in HRA's conference room. But what amazed him were the mannerisms of PAC representatives in high volume. Tony Scallon, PAC's chairperson, was known for his occasional volatile but well-strategized outbursts, which complemented Swanson's consistent controlled verbal hammering. Jack Cann, an activist in many causes (Jack probably would not like the word "cause"—too kumbaya for him) became a politically explosive Mick Jagger, moving around the table and shouting, according to Rudi, what were highly volatile but intelligent points of attack that could pull and keep the debate toward PAC positions. "Jack made Tony look like a moderate," Rudi commented.[35]

CHARLIE WARNER: THE "DOUBLE AGENT"

The Chicago Area HUD office oversaw the Minneapolis and St. Paul HUD-assisted operations. An employee in charge of this management was Charlie Warner, who came to the Twin Cities often to coordinate activities with the Minneapolis HRA. Warner provided many poignant comments about the nature of the HUD leadership culture and his ensuing relationship with PAC:

> *Administrating an area-based urban renewal plan that intended to cover many blocks of a city area was a challenging task. They were compiled to include not only all properties to be subject to the plan but also conditions of the buildings, real estate information and very extensive components such as relocation, legal status, infrastructure information, etc. The application of city and state laws could be confusing and contradictory. At many points, decisions had to be made to administer various components of the plan. HRA would write to me in HUD's Chicago office for interpretations from time to time.*[36]

In his late twenties, with a degree in classics and an MBA, Charlie was one of several new hires in HUD who took part in what he described as a "perfect storm"—being in the right place at the right time to dedicate themselves to President Lyndon Johnson's Great Society program. Charlie and his cohorts called themselves "Concerned HUD Employees," or CHE—a tongue-in-cheek reference to the Cuban revolutionary guerrilla brother of Fidel Castro. In this milieu, he said, "There was idealism even by top leaders who sought to do genuine public good."

When Charlie was in Minneapolis, he enjoyed neighborhood meetings. In Northeast Minneapolis, many citizens distrusted and feared government, influenced by their anticommunism, as many of them were immigrants from Russia and eastern bloc countries. Seward West soon attracted Charlie, who exclaimed, "Seward West PAC was fun!"

Charlie began to see that the HRA South Area Office was not operating its renewal program in Seward West in accordance with how it was intended to be carried out. One of the problems was HRA's extreme reluctance to engage in citizen participation, which was an important component for HUD. He also saw Seward West PAC's considerable depth of knowledge of how urban renewal was supposed to work. So, in Warner's words, he "flipped" and surreptitiously slipped critical information to PAC, sending in advance to PAC his interpretations of urban renewal policy HRA was asking for. "When I sent PAC the HRA-intended information, I knew PAC would open their mail the next day, while HRA would take several days to read theirs," he said. "So this gave PAC plenty of time to gear up before HRA knew what was in store for them."[37]

A-LIST AND B-LIST HOUSES

When New York City Hall scheduled Jane Jacob's West Greenwich Village for a demolition-based urban renewal plan based on area-wide blight, Jacobs and her neighbors organized the Save the West Village Committee. This group of nonprofessional citizens worked to disprove blighting conditions by conducting a neighborhood-wide housing survey of housing units and compiling an inventory based on unit square footage, bathrooms, kitchens, number of occupants and rent amount.[38]

In Seward West, PAC acknowledged blight and formed a citizen-based survey crew to determine the level of physical condition was moderate

This photograph presents a typical pre-renewal view of houses that were dramatically altered from their original 1880s construction.

enough to make rehabilitation economically feasible. In 1972, a team of PAC members conducted a house-by-house preliminary survey of most of the single-family and multi-unit structures in the thirty-five-block Seward West area to assess their potential for rehab. Most of the observations were based solely on exteriors, but many residents allowed and even welcomed the team into their houses. The team analyzed and categorized each house in terms of apparent structural condition, degree of exterior repair, number of bedrooms and other factors. PAC team members had one or two people with general architectural or construction expertise who could describe observed conditions. Other team members were able to learn the basics of evaluation as they conducted the survey in order to form group decisions. From a technical standpoint, the team members were inexperienced in housing rehabilitation. In this way, however, PAC reflected the incomplete and untrained rehab knowledge of almost all housing experts and builders dominating the housing market.

The preliminary survey provided PAC with a real-life orientation to deal with the issues that greatly contributed to their working process. In particular, this survey eventually enabled PAC to develop a rehab policy that became a fundamental framework for both HRA and PAC to formulate joint discussions on house rehab feasibility and, eventually, some mutual decisions. But before that could happen, HRA had to decide whether to sit down with PAC and discuss a fundamental aspect underpinning the basis for its renewal plan. And if HRA chose to discuss this issue, it would imply that both sides would have to agree on the final disposition of this preliminary survey.

PAC's method was to cull out houses in HRA's "Definite Acquisition" category (meaning to be demolished after acquisition), which PAC's survey judged to have no potential for rehabilitation. That compilation was called the "A list"—those homes to be demolished without dispute. All other houses formed the "B list." The criteria for the B-list properties was that they possessed some possibility for rehab and thus deserved a classification to protect them until additional examination could determine their final disposition, whether that be rehab or demolition. Through considerable political pressure, HRA agreed to meet with PAC on the A and B lists.

On August 15, 1972, five days after intense negotiations, PAC held a special meeting to present the proposed A and B lists to the public of Seward West. In addition to the PAC board, those present included two South Area Office HRA staff members, ward alderman Zollie Green and two members of a short-lived PAC opposition group, the Seward West Homeowners Association. At the beginning of the session, Tony Scallon convinced Second Ward alderman John Cairns to oversee PAC-HRA negotiations on the issue. PAC proposed the A and B list: A-list would be those PAC agreed could be demolished, while B-list houses would be considered for rehab feasibility. The main commentators on the issue were PAC president Lowell Johnson, Tony Scallon, Legal Aid attorney Steve Swanson, PAC members Sally

Thomas and Don Barton and HRA South Area director Jack Crimmins (who was still in place at this time). A partial account of the minutes of that meeting reads as follows:

Tony: "This is what we came up with after 1½ hours of hot and heavy negotiations. Alderman John Cairns was there for assistance to both sides. PAC would prefer a language change [to the HRA renewal plan], *but the basic agreement is to go with this policy of disposition on definite acquisition. We have lists A and B. Exhibit A is to be acquired and cleared, and exhibit B is to be resurveyed. This was reached through bargaining. We had to give up something to get this, so we gave north of Franklin and west of Minnehaha except 4 parcels on Block 1 and 1914 East 22ⁿᵈ Street. Owners who strongly expressed that they want to stay were recognized. The policy allows for owners who want to sell* [to HRA]. *The finalized wording is close to done but not finished. This may have accomplished the completion of negotiations. Some houses we'll never agree on, but let's start the basic disagreements after the plan is started."*

Steve passed out the revised policy, and everyone took time to read it.

Tony: "This policy would be adopted by the HRA commissioners and will end there. They will be the enforcers. No prior agreement with HUD has been reached. The reason HUD doesn't want it put in the plan or contract is because HUD legal counsel has indicated they won't go along with that. This policy allows for a greater survey than HUD would go along with. This is just a promise. It can be retracted as easily as its adopted. Commissioners are the only enforcers. It is good in that it provides for a wide scope of resurvey except north of Franklin and west of Minnehaha. The execution is outlined in the policy."

When PAC was ready to make a motion approving the new policy, Don Barton said: "I keep swaying. One minute I think its great, and other times I'm not so sure. In some ways it's more than we ever thought possible, and in some ways it's not so much because it's not enforceable. It's not over now. We're going to have to be strong and stay together for the next three years."

Jack Crimmins: "I was able to get a hold of the HUD area counsel this afternoon, and he said he thought it sounded acceptable to HUD and said I could say that here."

Steve: "HUD's position is hands off. Sure, HUD is going to be happy with this policy because they don't have to enforce it. They may say tough bananas when we run into trouble later. We could run this over to them now, but they might reject it. Once we lose the HUD handle, we lose a lot."

Tony: "I'm a moderate and would prefer to work on the four-block area and owners who want to stay. This is the only way to get a broad survey."

Sally Thomas: "Is a massive resurvey necessary?"

Tony: "Don says yes. I say no."

Don: "I don't think it's massive."

Lowell: "Would someone like to re-phrase Sally's question? I'll rephrase Sally's question. Is a survey of all 181 structures necessary? [181 was the number of houses in the definite acquisition category.]

Roll was called: Yes, 12; Abstain, 1 [Alice Olson]. *The motion passed.*

Lowell: "We will recommend this policy, as revised, to the commissioners."[39]

The HRA commissioners subsequently approved the A and B lists, and HUD never called it into question. The A list thus provided a sense of agreement with HRA on a fundamental component of its renewal policy. For PAC, it stripped away the most dilapidated houses and allowed it to focus on a more concentrated segment of B-list properties. Both organizations then set up a procedure by which HRA would notify PAC of upcoming demolitions of A-list houses that essentially became consent items.

PAC's struggle with HRA achieved an important victory in the summer of 1972. A *Minneapolis Star Tribune* article dated Friday, August 18, of that year noted, "[PAC] won an 18-month battle Thursday when a city agency agreed to take another look at plans to demolish one-third of the district's homes." The article continued, "The revised policy approved unanimously yesterday by the Minneapolis Housing and Redevelopment Authority (HRA) calls for a review of demolition plans for 181 buildings, about half the number originally scheduled for demolition." The newspaper described how, several months earlier, PAC had persuaded then-senator Donald Fraser to visit Milwaukee Avenue during a PAC-arranged visit to see for

This pre-renewal photograph of 2108 Milwaukee Avenue shows the home's original asphaltic shingle siding, Italianate-style second-floor window hoods and oculus attic window.

himself the street's unique character. The A and B lists gave PAC another pragmatic strategy, as the group could now appear to be both tough and reasonable—tough because it could further harden its hardcore position on rehab and reasonable because it exhibited a measure of realism.

The A- and B-list houses became the backbone of land disposition recognized as policy by both HRA and PAC. This made possible the future Individual Rehab program, which eventually converted many B-list houses from their former demolition classification to rehabilitated dwellings and changed the entire physical character of the neighborhood. And its most special outcome was saving Milwaukee Avenue.

Sometime later, an undated letter from Thomas Feeney, director of the Minneapolis–St. Paul HUD office, to Robert Dronen, executive director of the Minneapolis HRA, confirmed a meeting with PAC on October 30, 1973. The letter intended to resolve how properties would be submitted through a local lending institution to HUD's single-family appraisal section, which attached conditions such as submitting a scope of work for the rehab and established value for insurance purposes. The most troublesome attached condition, however, was Item A, which stated that "the maximum limit on rehabilitation would not exceed 75% of estimated market resale price less the estimated marketable resale value less the established land reuse value if cleared."

The problem here was that the Seward West rehab was expected to easily—in fact, significantly—exceed a total of 75 percent of the resale value. HRA's renewal program had set a very minimal price for land value, and rehab costs were based on massive reconstruction costs, not the typical patch-and-paint remodeling costs of middle-class neighborhoods. It was this factor that caused HRA to peg 70 percent of properties to be acquired for demolition when the Seward West Renewal Program was written, well before its implementation.

Thankfully, by 1974, the mayor's office in Minneapolis had foreseen this situation and developed the rehab write-down program, which subsidized the margin of rehab costs that exceeded HUD's formula (to be discussed later.)

CHAPTER 10
PAC Gains a Political Victory

*I think this younger generation has got something to say to us, and I'm not sure
that what they say all the time is necessarily the final word. I always believed in
the right of a person to speak. I don't think he always has the right to be taken
seriously, but he ought to have a right to say what he wants to say.*
—*Hubert Humphrey, quoted in Robert Goodman's* After the Planners

That negotiated agreement with HRA gave PAC a bona fide role in the renewal program's operation. In utterly practical terms, this meant that PAC could butt heads with HRA on a somewhat uneven playing field, but at least it was out of the bleachers and on the same turf as HRA. More specifically, PAC gained acceptance to HRA's South Area Office, where HRA staff members administered the Seward West Renewal Program. Conveniently located just a few blocks away was the PAC office, where PAC's five-person staff worked and coordinated day-to-day activities. The PAC office was soon frequented regularly by Minneapolis City Council members, as well as Tom Johnson of the Second Ward and Zollie Green of the Ninth Ward, both representing Seward West, although divided by a north–south ward boundary line running down the middle of Milwaukee Avenue—a seemingly small bit of political geography that eventually came to work in PAC's advantage. This evolving status also brought many interested observers to visit PAC's office and attend its meetings. Students with classes in political science and urban studies, some staff members in city and state government and activists in various housing-based community organizations came to

An architect and prospective homeowner meet at the PAC office to review drawings.

gain knowledge of how a neighborhood urban renewal program was being reshaped by this group of citizen-activists.

A main function of the PAC relocation staff was answering residents' questions about wanting to stay in their houses or the need to relocate after their houses had been purchased by HRA. Unlike the formalized bureaucratic promulgations coming from HRA, PAC's response was very personal and spoken as directly as the residents could relate to, with conversations about neighborhood relationships that dated back a few generations.

Jeri Reilly realized that a very important aspect of this was that a history of the people who were the backbone of Milwaukee Avenue, from its origins to the present, came into focus. In a short time, those residents' recollections outlined a poignant sketch of how the tight little area around Milwaukee Avenue represented a history worth recording and contributing to a historic district centered on the street.

Milwaukee Avenue as Urban Ecology

PAC staff began to increase focus on Milwaukee Avenue for its well-worn aesthetic and, more importantly, its potential to be rescued as a model of urban ecology. At PAC meetings, staff members expounded about its compact living environment and recycling existing structures to create energy-efficient homes close to many urban amenities. Its location abutting Franklin Avenue and its three bus lines also provided transit alternatives.

Historic importance did not factor in analysis. A modicum of homage by the public at this time focused on prevailing standards of architectural history—cathedrals, college halls of learning, massive public buildings and other edifices that were markers of recorded history and culture. The architecture of fancy mansions was of no interest to PAC, nor was the destruction of the magnificent Romanesque Metropolitan building in downtown Minneapolis a decade before.

PAC staff made a photographic inventory of many of the houses on Milwaukee Avenue and some of the nearby houses on Twenty-second and Twenty-third Avenues. Recorded in the inventory were the physical conditions of exteriors, degrees of alteration and structures that might not have potential for rehab. Very gradually, and without realizing it, the architecture of the street's houses became more appealing. While they had first been viewed as individual structures, they were now being looked at in terms of their ability to become greater than the sum of their parts—a continuous architectural environment.

The concept of a pedestrian walkway (PAC did not call it a mall then) to replace the narrow outmoded street quickly became an important concept for PAC. After the landscaped walkway became a PAC-approved concept, when PAC members and staff would first mention to their neighbors about saving the houses from demolition, they would hear them say, "You know what you should think about? Tearing up that narrow street and building a mall—for people, not cars. It's the natural thing to do, you know."

Such collective thinking occurred with other transformational changes happening in and around the neighborhood. Collective thinking in the years 1972–74 produced Seward Co-op Grocery and Seward Co-op Childcare in Seward West; Peoples' Clothes, a clothing co-op nearby on Franklin Avenue in the Phillips neighborhood; and the Freewheel Bike Cooperative, North Country Co-op Grocery and North Country Hardware on the West Bank. Community health clinics operating outside mainstream medical practice but were supported by the professionals who had chosen to work for the low-income and disadvantaged people. These cooperative-run enterprises were preceded in Seward West as well as nearby neighborhoods by cooperative housing arrangements that at the time were called communes.

PAC RESHAPES PLANS FOR SEWARD WEST

An early exercise in land planning came with a number of contiguous A-list properties mixed with houses of rehab potential slated for clearance in a two-block area in the southeastern part of Seward West. HRA's plan listed the entire two blocks for demolition. The major reason was a long-standing HUD and HRA policy of clearing an entire block of houses if 50 percent had been found to lack rehab potential, even if the other houses on that block were judged capable of rehab. Prior to Seward West, many renewal areas in other cities experienced whole-block demolition, resulting in sizeable areas being chopped out of traditional neighborhoods and providing opportunity for developers to build new apartment buildings or rows of new featureless houses that were out of scale and design when compared to the surrounding traditional houses. Their identical design smacked of public housing, or "projects," that degraded surrounding traditional neighborhood streetscapes. These HRA planning exercises occasionally created a stigma of undervaluing what made a traditional neighborhood, affecting social stability as well as real estate values.

PAC saw this area as an opportunity, an important step in redeveloping the Seward West neighborhood. Both PAC and HRA agreed that the dilapidated A-list houses in this two-block area were beyond any chance of rehabilitation. HRA had no vision for what type of redevelopment should occur in what would become open sites, but PAC was anxious to ensure that housing appropriate to the needs of a family-oriented neighborhood and designed to integrate with existing single-unit houses could remain.

PAC staff put its site-planning expertise to work and designed an overall schematic site plan for these two blocks that emphasized rehab of stable existing houses while constructing new adjacent town houses on several parcels of combined open lots. PAC met with HRA South Area Office staff during the design phase and gradually provided input. As a result, the term "new construction infill" came into use to describe areas containing new housing units architecturally designed to complement and fit alongside existing houses on adjacent or nearby lots. New construction infill, PAC believed, could be appropriately designed to maintain the overall character of the neighborhood.

At this point, the long-standing HRA-PAC fight was interrupted by mutual understanding and agreement on the viability of the East Twenty-fourth Street plan. HRA contacted Williams O'Brien Architects, a local firm with experience in design for urban renewal areas. With PAC review, the firm designed several clusters of infill town houses that were built and mixed in with existing houses. The units were mildly contemporary in terms of architectural design, with general forms and proportions that accommodated nearby rehabilitated houses. But that accommodation in itself was some measure of success for both sides. HRA could claim progress in achieving quality development of parcels within the renewal area, and PAC could measure its expertise in practical and innovative planning for its neighborhood, proving to HRA that the group was both pragmatic and imaginative and an able agent in urban renewal problem solving. More important, however, was the fact that public agencies changed their policies regarding whole-block demotion. Adding to this breakthrough rather than developing a whole block with housing structures designed to ignore its residential surroundings, the concept of infill new construction designed to fit within a traditional neighborhood entered the urban scene in Minneapolis for the first time.

Nonetheless, the HRA South Area Office continued to maintain a policy of steadfastly exercising a dominant position in administration of the area's renewal actions while begrudgingly accepting some kind of meaningful working relationship with PAC.

Sometime afterward, at an HRA board meeting, commissioners excitedly announced that a Minneapolis architectural firm had contacted the agency for approval to perform a quick study of Milwaukee Avenue to rehab its houses under a Federal Section 236 subsidized rental program. HRA agreed, and PAC was ecstatic. The study was slow to start, and just after it did, President Richard Nixon announced suspension of the Section 236 subsidized program. The architects quickly withdrew. Other proposals came forth from time to time; a presenter would make a verbal description of a plan to save Milwaukee Avenue at a PAC meeting, but nothing of substance would follow.

An imperceptible aspect to the possible but not yet determinable development of Milwaukee Avenue at this time began to emerge. The developers who came and went reportedly realized after a closer view of the scope of the development that a sizable amount of time was needed to sort things out, to determine what was yet vastly undeterminable. The bottom line for developers was that their front-end costs made involvement beyond their normal speculative considerations too risky. This factor necessary for development of Milwaukee Avenue became apparent—that length of time PAC subconsciously began to realize its planning expertise could afford to do. Moreover, also unknown at that time was that this unconventional development project had a knowledgebase that only PAC and HRA had in their heads, making them the un-anointed and seemingly unlikely development option.

At a meeting a few months earlier, on February 8, 1973, Jack Crimmins of HRA, Ralph Quiggle of the City Planning Department and Don Erickson of Building Inspections had discussed the A and B lists. Recorded in the minutes of the meeting was the following: "There are 40 such A-list houses in the Milwaukee Avenue area and many more B-list houses which HRA feels should be torn down." The administrators then discussed the cost of rehab and its problems. The following was noted in the minutes of the meeting:

> *The possibility of gutting the structures was discussed. Don Erickson (building inspector) thought the buildings were probably of balloon framing construction and that the 2x4 wall framing extending from the first-floor members alongside the second-floor framing continuously upward to support roof rafters would, in this case, "all collapse if this were done." Problems of meeting building code were talked about, and Erickson added, "The minimum lot width is 40 feet. There is a 10% maximum variation from the building code. The railroad houses would require over that maximum to meet the code. All of the houses are at present legal nonconforming houses."[40]*

A short time later, Ralph Quiggle submitted a report on the meeting to the Minneapolis Heritage Preservation Commission, stating that an outcome of the meeting was a directive to the city's inspection department to conduct a voluntary inspection of eight houses on Milwaukee Avenue. The houses would be selected by PAC, and HRA would interpret the results in terms of cost and financial feasibility. Quiggle's report to the HPC noted that a study of the area's history was needed but that "HRA was not equipped to do this sort of thing." Asked by a commissioner if the Minnesota Historical Society "had done anything on this," Charlie Nelson, MHS's historical architect and the man who would eventually guide a successful historic designation process, replied that Brooks Cavin, one of the first architects in the early

1970s to develop the foundations for Minnesota's initial historic preservation movement, would undertake the study. The study never happened. Meanwhile, the PAC-HRA battle continued.

PAC CHANGES FOCUS, RELOCATION BEGINS

For those of us who were new residents for whom "time swept us into place," the eventual and inevitable relocation of older longtime residents, who had in the early '70s sought to fight being forced out of their houses, became swept out of place.

They became out of place when their houses no longer embraced their longstanding way of life. In other words, what had been conditions of bare living, long taken for granted, no longer fit the overall scheme of an about-to-be renewed neighborhood. For many, the meagerness of their standard of living was the result of minimal income. Several, however, had average-wage jobs, and a few were skilled workers with substantial incomes. What tied them to this area is that it was the place where they were born and had grown up. They were close to relatives and longtime friends but lacked a greater awareness, being isolated from their middle-class neighbors. By this time, however, they were beginning to understand their changing circumstances. These longtime residents came to this realization that they had to adjust their lives to a yet unknown ledge in some socioeconomic level, perhaps a lower rung of the middle class. How that was to happen soon became apparent.

Providentially, they overcame their distrust of HRA and realized that the agency actually offered a policy by which they could purchase a house at fair market value, something that was previously unavailable to them. Moreover, HRA's purchase offer was coupled with a seemingly generous bonus of $15,000 in grant-free money just to allow HRA to buy their houses, plus providing for moving expenses.

Those indecipherable HRA letters to Seward West relocatees became understandable when PAC's three-person relocation staff was able to communicate clearly the intent and procedures of HRA. After the Berget family on Twenty-third Avenue successfully completed their paperwork and title transfer to HRA and moved into a house in the nearby suburb of Apple Valley, it made relocation a reality for others. The previous second-hand information that past HRA renewal programs had forced people out of their houses with little compensation was now inoperative. The Bergets had been part of an extended family along Twenty-third Avenue, and soon other kinfolk were set to move. Those older residents who once vowed to "chase those bureaucrats away" now sat in front of an HRA bureaucrat's desk and mentioned how they would like to move before winter because their space heaters barely got them through the last one or because a roof leak just wouldn't stop despite their brother-in-law's patch job.

On Milwaukee Avenue and in the other blocks throughout Seward West, house after house became vacant and boarded as the owners moved out. The HRA acquisition that PAC once fought against now became a critical mechanism in PAC's plan to redevelop the Milwaukee Avenue houses. HRA, however, still remained unconvinced. Unseen and unmeasured, PAC switched gears; it was no longer fighting to keep residents in their homes by forestalling demolition and finding ways to help them rehabilitate them, which only a few were interested in doing. PAC's evolved strategy became developing various ways in which it could save the neighborhood by rehabilitating the houses for new owners, who gradually became the emerging class of the young counterculture.

The turnover of houses from private ownership to HRA was gradual, due in part to the agency's slow-moving administrative apparatus. The effect

A vacant and boarded-up house at 2125 Milwaukee Avenue.

was beneficial, however, avoiding the shock of many houses in all parts of the neighborhood becoming vacant, with painted plywood covering the windows. On Milwaukee Avenue, the effect of vacant houses was more pronounced. Now that special ambience created by the closeness of the houses served to underscore its vacancies, as the neighborhood became a deserted place.

Having nearly all of the Milwaukee Avenue houses vacant was advantageous for both HRA and PAC. The agency, still feeling it held all the cards, saw an empty neighborhood as a catalyst to clear-cutting the area when the time was right. PAC used the opportunity to more closely study the houses for rehab potential. By this time, HRA's familiarity with PAC staff members led to the latter's status as trusted functionaries—a few of us were given master keys for the houses' padlocks.

What Was Left Behind

Our daughter Carla, a preschooler when we lived on Milwaukee Avenue, remembers finding a turquoise Fiesta saucer among assorted dishware when she and her kindergarten-aged playmates snuck into the vacant houses on Milwaukee Avenue. She was happy to give it to my wife, Sally, and it is still stacked with other Fiesta saucers in our kitchen cabinets today. By 1974, many of the street's houses had been vacated of their former occupants, and lives once lived in these places had disappeared—except for miscellaneous remnants of what was left behind. Wandering through these houses was a childhood pursuit for Carla and her friends, discovery by their own initiative. Out of sight from adults, their adventures occasionally led to finding oddments such as kitchen utensils, well-worn clothing and forgotten or broken toys, which they were excited to take home (especially bedraggled dolls) to extend a few moments of enjoyment before they were thrown away and lost forever.

What seemed surprising to her was the range of conditions in these interiors. Some were broom-clean, with no trace elements to offer her and her friends clues of the lives of those who moved away. They may have been people like the Joads in Steinbeck's *The Grapes of Wrath*, the Oklahomans who packed some curios and other personal objects into their trucks before moving to California "so we can still know we are us."

In their mysterious silences, these houses stored memories, Carla said recently, and sometimes she felt a set of dishes could tell her stories. Some houses had large peace symbols painted on the walls. Others told vignettes all too well: extremely worn-out furniture and incredibly food-stained kitchen stoves were telltale signs of the disorder and utter meagerness of these families. Some houses, as those of us on the planning team also discovered, were trashed, with debris everywhere. But why? We didn't know what those stories could be.

The moving of these longtime Milwaukee Avenue residents, relocated by the city's urban renewal process, took place over a two-year period. What this meant for Carla was a decreasing number of friends with whom she could wander into soon-to-be-diminished places of childhood wonder.

CHAPTER 11

Milwaukee Avenue Planning Moves Forward

A rebel loves a cause.
—*Joni Mitchell, "Don't Interrupt the Sorrow"*

The disposition of Milwaukee Avenue increased as a standoff issue between PAC and HRA. The agency's contention that the houses were in an extreme state of dilapidation was exacerbated by what it called "planning reasons." Milwaukee Avenue's substandard lot sizes did not meet zoning, and there were no front yards or viable walkways.

For PAC and HRA, Milwaukee Avenue was a physical entity very comprehensible and easily defined enough to be an attractive argument. This factor fed into it becoming a strategic imperative for each side to win. HRA's perceptions of Milwaukee Avenue's unorthodox conditions made PAC look like the extremists the agency sought to paint them to be. PAC had its own strategic reason to fight for the street, as its definable characteristics knit together a cogent entity with which PAC, not yet familiar with historic preservation, felt best equipped to take on HRA. Moreover, for some (but not all) PAC members, the HRA's reasons to obliterate the street were the very reasons they wanted to save it.

But for the PAC membership at large, at least subconsciously, Milwaukee Avenue evoked a physical attractiveness that became its romantic education. The narrow street and the houses close up to it provided an intimate scale, and the brick houses with gingerbread porches evoked a charm that the oncoming generation could love.

THE MILWAUKEE AVENUE FOUR-BLOCK-AREA PLANNING TEAM

PAC's hardheaded tactics during its constant encounters with HRA were useful. Nonetheless, PAC, now focusing on Milwaukee Avenue, saw the need to group together a few HRA staffers whose personalities allowed reasoned discussion to delineate what the two organizations could agree on and then work out differences to form a rational method and planning procedures. Jeri Reilly and I proposed to ask two HRA representatives to meet on a regular basis, our purpose being to decide whether Milwaukee Avenue could be saved and on what basis a redevelopment plan could be formulated.

Bill Schatzlein, a mild-mannered HRA South Area Office planner, and Bob Scroggins, a well-humored and engaging assistant area director, agreed to form the team. Schatzlein and Scroggins saw the need to resolve conflict issues as an important part of the mission of the agency. We PAC staffers believed our cause was right—and eventually would accomplish the daunting task of saving the street. However, Jeri and I agreed that finding the solution had to be developed by a dispassionate study of relevant factors and that this was a case to set aside PAC ideology.

The PAC-HRA study group was named the Milwaukee Avenue Four-Block-Area Planning Team. The four blocks facing Milwaukee Avenue—the east side of Twenty-second Avenue and the west side of Twenty-third Avenue—contained houses and lots with much in common with Milwaukee Avenue, especially the somewhat larger Twenty-second Avenue houses. Geographically, the four-block area boundaries were Franklin Avenue at the north, Twenty-third Avenue to the east, East Twenty-fourth Street to the south and Twenty-second Avenue to the west. Overall land size was 6.5 residential acres. The land was relatively flat, with a slight continuous north–south slope downward from Franklin Avenue to its southern terminus. The four members of the team formulated Milwaukee Avenue study objectives:

> *General Objectives:*
> *To retain the existing character of architectural style, visual image, scale of buildings, and historic era.*
> *To provide safe, sound, and marketable housing.*
> *To provide sufficient amenities and conveniences consistent with #1 above, to accommodate contemporary residential needs and standards.*
> *To the extent feasible, provide housing within the economic range of the current residents of the Seward West area.*

Development Objectives:
The development shall consist of a maximum of 22 dwelling units per acre.
The right-of-way of Milwaukee Avenue shall be maintained.
The development shall consist of the rehab of as many Milwaukee Avenue houses as possible, while meeting other objectives.

In order to retain as much of the original character as possible, the rehabilitated structures shall be in groups rather than scattered. This does not exclude the retention of isolated structures.

Sufficient side yards or other means shall be provided to reduce fire hazards and provide for adequate light, ventilation, and ease of maintenance.

Site development and housing units should be designed to accommodate a variety of households.

New housing shall be single family, semi-detached, or town houses. Walk-up apartments shall be excluded.

One off-street parking place per unit shall be provided and located as close as possible to the individual units.

Private yard space shall be provided for each unit.

These planning objectives were primarily written by PAC staff, with additional input by Bob Scroggins and Bill Schatzlein for zoning conformance. Many of the provisions directly reflect PAC fundamental philosophy, the foremost being providing affordable housing to the extent possible and the organization's longstanding aversion to apartment buildings as destructive to the neighborhood. Keeping Milwaukee Avenue as an open space, no matter the outcome of the rehab question, was highly desired. But we focused very intently on the issue of grouping rehabilitated houses to preserve the houses' predominant importance—working together as multiple elements essential to the street's architectural character.

Missing from these directives was examination of historic preservation as an appropriate tool in the rehab process. There were two reasons for this omission: (1) PAC was so keenly pressed into the legitimacy of the issue in its abstract consideration and (2) PAC wanted to keep historic designation off the table for reasons of subterfuge that will be revealed later.

On April 26, 1973, PAC adopted the Milwaukee Avenue study objectives. The planning team stated progress reports would be presented to PAC at every meeting. Discussion was always extensive, with PAC board members keeping their remarks at an informative level. Away from meetings, meeting PAC members here and there in the neighborhood or at Saturday night parties, discussion of the planning study became an acceptable topic of social conversation.

The 100 housing structures in the four-block area contained 145 dwelling units, mostly single-unit houses, with several duplexes facing Milwaukee Avenue and two fourplexes facing East Twenty-fourth Street. A total of forty-six single-family and duplex structures faced Milwaukee Avenue. The planning team agreed the complete four-block land tract should be studied, as a majority of its houses on and off Milwaukee Avenue fit the general architectural profiles and lot size characteristics. The unique presence and possible historic aspect of the Milwaukee Avenue houses meant more focus would be placed on them. Any proposed mix of rehab and new housing—or all new housing, if it came to that—should maintain the same density and, to the extent possible, the same lot line configurations unless new town houses would be proposed as infill housing. The existing uniform setback off the public right of way must be strictly maintained. Most important: the existing twenty-five-foot-wide street should be converted into a pedestrian walkway.

At this point, the PAC staff gained a new planner, John Wicks, a student in the University of Minnesota School of Architecture who was assigned by the school to work with us. He immediately fit in to our professional mode, such as it was, that the PAC office had established and began to work on a variety of Seward West projects. He quickly understood the complicated four-block-area design issues and became a very adept architectural staff member.

The next move for the planning team was formulating a three-stage plan that would determine future development and decide whether that development would include the all-important issue of feasible and marketable rehab. The first phase was collecting the relevant information, reviewing the PAC conceptual site plan and, most importantly, devising a methodology to analyze rehab study criteria. Phase two was to perform rehab analysis and potential for new infill to replace houses incapable of rehabilitation. The team would study the concept to rezone the area with a new zoning mechanism: planned residential development, or PRD. Results of sampling a selected number of houses that could be candidates for rehab would determine the decision to save or demolish Milwaukee Avenue, although without setting a minimum number of houses. A four-block area development-based site plan would establish a property-by-property disposition and site design features. Phase three would involve adjusting the four-block-area plan for continuing site and property analysis, seeking out a potential developer for certain areas and developing a method for marketing the houses.

Before this time, several PAC leaders had apprehensively discussed openly among themselves how rehab feasibility for the Milwaukee Avenue houses would be determined. Full-scale house rehab was not operating in the housing construction market. By exterior appearances, many of the houses seemed to be in very deteriorated condition. But their overall exterior envelope and square footage was less than those of typical houses, which seemed to imply lower rehab costs.

But floor-area square footage is, at best, a rough method to estimate construction costs. Instead, the major method we used to estimate these costs was analyzing an approximate ratio of cubic feet within the building shell to the square feet of all exterior and interior wall areas as well as floor areas. A ratio with cubic feet and surface area within a relatively close ratio would mean the building contained a considerable amount of exterior and interior wall surfaces that might have a significant construction cost, while ratio numbers with a wider spread would imply a more efficient design in terms of construction cost. Simply put, a square box empty of interior walls would cost less to build than a similar sized shape containing many interior walls.

What the typical Milwaukee Avenue houses had going for them was a highly efficient design: a simple and compact exterior form with just enough interior walls to define their simple floor plans. In the end, this not-so-apparent efficient design made their rehab more feasible. We also used component costs, such as complete replacement of heating, plumbing and electrical systems, based on recommended estimates by the few contractors now working in the Seward West area, as well as contractors known by HRA construction specialists.

Several building contractors with some remodeling experience provided us with limited assistance. Remodeling consists of repairing knowable components, such as window glass, porch railings and other visible elements. Whole-house rehab, however, which is what these houses required, dealt with multiple interrelated problems not visible to the untrained eye, making cost estimating difficult and requiring an analytic method to diagnose hidden issues. As a result, this entire rehab feasibility issue was fraught with knowing and dealing with inexact data.

At this time, we became aware of Soderberg Construction, which was rehabilitating a row of elegant Victorian houses in splendid fashion in the Ramsey Hill area of St. Paul. From time to time, we would stop by a house on which Ron Soderberg and his father were working, and we quickly learned Ron's intelligence of his craft. Unlike every other contractor cast

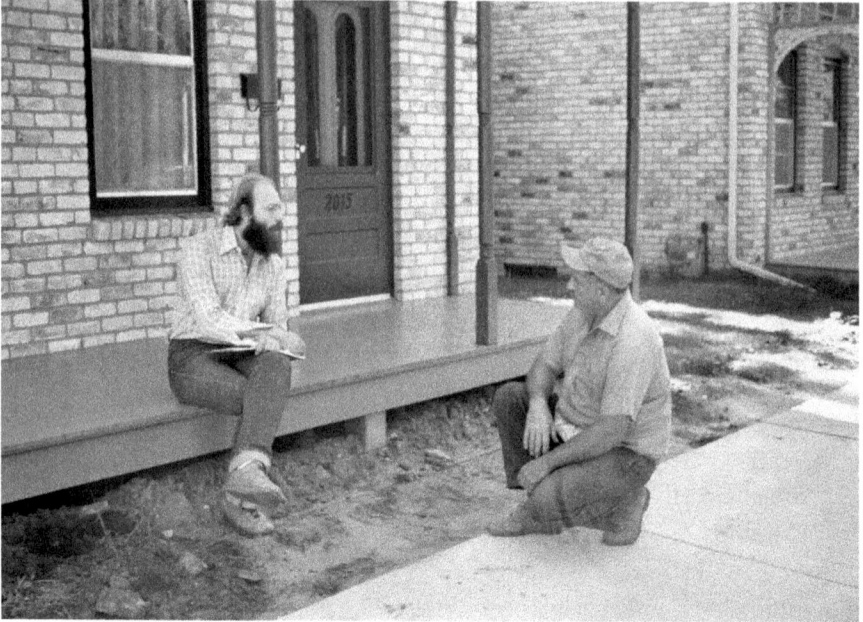

Ron Soderberg (left) and Mark Morris. Ron was owner of Soderberg Construction Company, which rehabilitated the first two packages of houses on Milwaukee Avenue and Twenty-second Avenue. Mark served as the project foreman.

in the stolid blue-collar mode, Ron was tall and slender, with long red hair and a trimmed beard. He was culturally in tune and gay, and his sparkling blue eyes and easy smile gave him an engaging manner. He knew about Milwaukee Avenue and its historic character, telling us how important it would be to restore those houses. A few years later, Ron would become a key figure in transforming the Milwaukee Avenue area.

How Few Houses?

The PAC planning team met with Tony and a few other key PAC leaders to consider the minimum number of rehab-feasible Milwaukee Avenue houses of the forty-four now existing (PAC had already allowed demolition of two houses) and what would it take to make saving a certain number of houses worthwhile. This bottom line became more complicated when we realized that some houses would have to be situated side by side—preferably

106

in clusters—in order to preserve the architectural continuity of the existing houses. This meant that if none of the feasible houses were aligned in pairs or larger clusters, the sense of continuity that defined Milwaukee Avenue would be lost; therefore, it might not be worth saving the street.

The team put these factors together, realizing that we were relying in part on an arbitrary factor to affect our decision. Of the forty-four existing houses, we started with a minimum number of sixteen, with a minimum of two clusters of existing houses. The minimum number of houses for each cluster, we thought, should be four. Could that minimum number of all the existing houses to be rehabilitated be fewer than sixteen? That answer didn't come right away, but it was the all-important one.

Team planners needed some visuals as well. From photographs we had taken, we had certain sets of particular houses that could form more definitive assessments. Their visual architectural alignment, coupled with the consideration of their conditions, began to affect our analysis. Thinking in images induced team members to place more study on specific clusters, which were identified and noted on rough preliminary site plans.

Our rehab analysis hinged on whether HRA would accept our study, as the agency had been building momentum all along to proceed with its original plan to demolish all of the Milwaukee Avenue houses. While our Milwaukee Avenue Four-Block-Area planning continued, Tony Scallon, Steve Swanson and other PAC leaders were engaging HRA and a few sympathetic council members with their political strategy to change how the overall renewal plan would be interpreted and administered.

STREET SMART: THINKING OF THE PEDESTRIAN WALKWAY

While addressing the rehab feasibility question, PAC team members were very attentive to what would happen with the street itself. This worn-out, uneven, narrow asphalt strip that seemed pressed against by the rows of houses on each side seemed to give us instructions on how to preserve its character.

As several former PAC members observed many years later, at that time, we knew we were way past operating within a normal framework, and this era of change gave us license to see the unorthodox as an antidote to the norm. As such, the whole idea of converting this obsolete street into a walkway was encapsulated into a simple thought: "Why not?" We knew this was a unique concept, but we were totally unaware that we were

This early sketch of part of the lower two blocks was used in studying the replacement of the existing narrow street with a pedestrian walkway.

forming what could become a model by which future neighborhoods could reclaim this very essence of livability—allowing neighbors to walk among each other without directing our footsteps out of the automobile traffic of the typical streets that form our neighborhoods. We possessed some sense that we were creating a historic district, but we were unaware that we were forming a historic construct that could serve as a future pattern for how city neighborhoods could be made more livable.

TIME FOR PROFESSIONAL PLANNING

In early 1973, the planning team decided that hiring architectural consultants for the considerable complexity of the area would be necessary, and that task required a professional consultant planner with the requisite skills and experience for the job. The selection proved to be a bit difficult. Only a small number of architectural firms in the early 1970s had working experience with city-sponsored projects, typically limited to designing new downtown office buildings on cleared HRA land. Moreover, community rehab-based planning was practically unknown—not only to architects but also to community organizations.

PAC recommended the architectural team of Stanley Fishman and Surendra Ahuja. Fishman, who combined his professional experience with his role as a design critic at the University of Minnesota School of Architecture, was known to have extensive experience with various St. Paul community projects incorporating community participation and city processes, usually in urban renewal contexts. He had a reputation among various community groups as a "people's architect." Fishman teamed with Surendra Ahuja, an urban design planner with city agency experience, and both were interviewed for the Milwaukee Avenue Four-Block-Area Plan. The pair was selected by a joint PAC-HRA decision. Fishman's engaging personality and apparent grasp of handling urban design problems set the process in motion with much excitement—and a lot of talking. He subtly rendered the impression with PAC representatives that he was in full understanding of the PAC viewpoint and began to frame study issues accordingly. Moreover, he knew how to talk housing rehab as if he had considerable experience in that area (obscuring the fact, as we later learned, that he didn't). The consultants' contract consisted of three main parts that followed the planning team's three-phase objectives. (Although we fired the consultants toward the end of the second phase.)

THE SECTION 236 TOWN HOUSES

Late on a Friday afternoon in 1973, Surendra Ahuja excitedly called me at work and told me his contacts at the local HUD office, which administered a federally subsidized rental housing program, Section 236, had just been notified that a housing developer was returning twelve vouchers for a cancelled housing construction program. Government regulations required the local office to turn the vouchers back to the Washington, D.C. headquarters after five days if they could not be reissued locally. Surendra asked me if I thought we could incorporate those twelve units somewhere on planned demolition sites at the south end of Milwaukee Avenue and elsewhere in Seward West.

First, we knew that five days—the following Tuesday—would give us a very tight deadline to put together application documents. While HUD staff could assemble the typical paperwork, our planning team and consultants had to quickly design schematic architectural documents such as a site plan, floor plans, elevations and preliminary specifications. At a bar near Surendra's office on Wabasha Street in downtown St. Paul, we began doing the typical architectural design doodling on bar napkins. We outlined a site with approximate dimensions between the south end of Milwaukee Avenue and Twenty-third Avenue and a second adjoining group of similarly sized lots across Twenty-third Avenue that contained four extremely dilapidated houses. Could both sites hold six units each, plus parking space and yard space to meeting zoning regulations? This was the type of planning with which Surendra was very talented, and his quick strokes on the napkins made everything fit. A quick call to Stan Fishman verified the footprint for the layout of town houses on the site plan. For Surendra and me, all that conceptual work was done in a little over an hour. But now a much more difficult and immediate task lay ahead.

I called Tony Scallon while Surendra and I were drinking and drawing. While I enthusiastically talked with Tony about the architectural breakthrough in the planning, he excitedly began to see its political implications. We quickly discussed what we had to do to get PAC approval, made very difficult due to an infighting contingent within PAC among staff members and some of the leaders planning the Milwaukee Avenue Four-Block Area. Later in the evening, Tony, myself and a likeminded PAC supporter met to lay out strategy. The next PAC meeting was scheduled well after the Tuesday deadline, but Tony and members of the PAC executive committee decided that they could act on behalf of the full membership.

The following day, Saturday morning, I hosted an impromptu meeting at my house, deliberately choosing both supporters and opponents. It was necessary to gain at least minimal acceptance by the opposition to ensure an eventual positive vote. Debate was very contentious, but having learned by this time how to read faces in a group about to vote on a contentious matter, I knew we held all the cards, and their arguments were based on opposition to our political status on the issue, not the issue itself. Tony informed the group when he counted votes of PAC members not present, plus supporters in the room, that the issue would carry. It was one thing to argue with Tony on issues (which he often invited), but nobody in the room would dispute his vote counting. More importantly, it was hard to argue against affordable housing development—the opposition group's main issue—especially when we could establish occupancy priority for Seward West families about to be relocated from their rental units in the neighborhood. After more debate, all present provided palpable agreement.

That afternoon, John Wicks and I met Stan Fishman at his architectural office with Surendra and the napkins. Stan had drawn some plans developed from our work and had just finished up some sketches. Some were what I would call "traditional modernism" and looked suspiciously like an affordable housing design Stan did along Concord Avenue in St. Paul, a thoroughfare that had scattered new town houses here and there but did not add up to a streetscape. We picked one of the schemes, which offered a series of somewhat low-pitched gables across the front and an irregular arrangement of windows. "They must have a twelve-by-twelve roof pitch," we said, "plus vertically oriented windows symmetrically ordered to balance with gable geometry." Stan grabbed his 8B pencil and some tracing paper and, with flourishing strokes, worked out several revisions. After more sketches and more of our remarks, the façades gained a compatible relationship with the nearby Milwaukee Avenue houses while also showing restraint in modern themes and ornamentation. In this way, these town houses could present themselves with the right kind of moderate background structures at the end of Milwaukee Avenue. By Tuesday, the application was in HUD's hands, with the South HRA Area Office in approval.

What came to be known as the Milwaukee Avenue Townhouses quickly became a huge accomplishment for PAC. Finding an obscure source of new-construction housing (of which HRA apparently was unaware) and getting HUD to approve construction in such quick order met many of PAC's goals and proved to everyone that PAC's pragmatic manner was to be taken seriously.

The construction cost for the twelve town house units, plus site costs, was $593,052, or $49,421 per unit. Under the Section 236 subsidized rental program, the occupants, who met specified eligibility requirements, paid rent as a percentage of their incomes.[41]

In mid-1975, the newly finished units stood proud as a significant accomplishment, both architecturally (as I had hoped) and politically (as Tony had envisioned). PAC and HRA ensured a specified number of the units were available for relocated neighborhood residents. PAC had proved that new architecture could become sympathetic infill—in this case within a later-to-be-determined historic environment. PAC also established itself as a contributor and not as an obstructionist to renewal of the community. HRA began to realize that PAC should be respected and would have to be reckoned with. The twelve town houses became one of PAC's successes in the physical outcome of Seward West.

In the immediate years after their construction, the town houses, based on their general form and primary architectural features, were widely seen as proper infill on Milwaukee Avenue. In later years, however, when it became perfectly acceptable, even by the gods and rulers of architecture, to once again attach ornament to new buildings, the public began to see them as slightly clumsy but with a benign presence. At least in a small sense, they now can be considered contributors to Milwaukee Avenue and a local architectural transitional development.

REHAB ANALYSIS OF SAMPLE MILWAUKEE AVENUE HOUSES

At the outset of phase one, PAC staff members had been working on rehab issues and the study of clusters as part of their duties within the planning team. They requested that the consultants study rehab feasibility of eight houses selected by them. Chosen were several houses on Milwaukee Avenue and two on Twenty-second Avenue that ranged in condition from severely dilapidated to apparently sound. These houses were visited on the exterior by Fishman and surveyed in the interior by PAC planning team members. Another set of houses was likewise surveyed.

Along Twenty-second Avenue South, eleven duplexes and five single-family houses were rehabilitated, while four new side-by-side duplexes were built to complement the existing structures.

PAC planning team members were guardedly optimistic that these rehab numbers on the first eight houses would eventually stand up with further review. Also, we still did not have more than an intuitive sense that an additional minimum eight houses would prove feasible. Almost surprisingly, our first estimates indicated that rehab was potentially workable. Our work and hopes had been going on for over two years, but where we were at this time was no cause for yelling out victory. So the next step was to present the current status at the next planning team meeting. Schatzlein and Scroggins were circumspect but had no objections, adding that more work was needed. PAC team members agreed, ever so subtly reinforcing their preliminary findings.

Scallon's political sledgehammer tactics, combined with his smooth behind-the-scenes finesse and the carefully measured temper of Swanson, more and more made PAC a forceful presence. In the 1973 Minneapolis council election campaign, Tony and his DFL young people had many PAC members knocking on doors and distributing campaign leaflets in four wards where four young DFL challengers were aiming to upset incumbents. The 1973 election swept all four into office, while Republican Tom Johnson, who had been very supportive of PAC, was reelected to the Second Ward, which represented much of Seward West. As a result, Scallon's political tactics served PAC's attempts to out-maneuver HRA's ability to get backing from city leaders. Was a breakthrough in the offing? Only an unorthodox move could allow such a transformation to occur.

CHAPTER 12

History Finally "Happens" on Milwaukee Avenue

The greatest quarterback sneak in 1974 did not happen on a football field. It took place in the office of the PAC when Jeri Reilly and I, as well as a few other PAC supporters and members, surreptitiously prepared a nomination form for Milwaukee Avenue's placement on the National Register of Historic Places. We were aided and abetted by Charlie Nelson, historical architect of the Minnesota Historical Society. Charlie had long championed our cause, and he saw a needed departure from the typical fare of what traditionally constituted historic importance, which back then was mainly limited to courthouses, prominent churches, sumptuous houses of important people and the architecturally resplendent places that marked the upper registers of society. Jeri's research on the immigrants' role was critically important for the nomination's merit. In her words, "[Milwaukee Avenue] is one of Minneapolis's few intact examples of the lifestyle of the poor immigrant who came to Minnesota when America was the New World. The narrow street, with its small lookalike houses tucked closely together, offers a visual lesson in economic and social history. It serves as striking contrast to those artifacts of aristocracy which are the normal fare of historic preservation."[42] Nelson added, "It's time America learned about how common people lived, sometimes with uncommon achievements."

PAC staff members didn't want to notify HRA about their intentions, fearing it would try to interfere, while Nelson was apprehensive about what the Minnesota Historical Society's review committee would think about including what he called "Joe Sixpack's" relevance to history. But the committee agreed with Nelson, and when the nomination was sent to the National Register, Milwaukee Avenue's eligibility gave it protection during the forty-five-day wait for the determination. The following morning, HRA officials had their breakfasts ruined when they read the *Minneapolis Star Tribune* article announcing Milwaukee Avenue's new historical status.

When the HRA staff got into their offices, they overreacted to the situation. As planned, HRA was caught completely unaware. When the nomination made the local newspapers, the agency quickly threw in the towel on the Milwaukee Avenue issue. But by this time, PAC had gained a tentative upper hand in all matters regarding Seward West renewal. Nonetheless, HRA's sudden reversal of course somehow seemed surprising, but the agency and PAC quickly made a seamless relationship of effortless cooperation. A day after the historic designation announcement, HRA's first phone message to PAC office staff was, "How can we help?"

As an undergraduate student majoring in American history, Jeri began to write her major paper, "Temporary Home: The Immigrant in Minneapolis, 1895–1910 (Milwaukee Avenue: A Case Study)." Her work required extensive research in the form of examining deed books and census tracts. State records contained what Jeri called a "treasure-trove" of personal information, including ethnic origins, occupations, number of persons in the household, etc. All of the information was handwritten, as these were the days before microfiche. Jeri painstakingly pored over deeds in the Hennepin County Courthouse files, which were also handwritten and included hand-scribed notations of dollar amounts of lot transactions. With all that information, she looked for patterns marking significant events. For instance, in 1890, a large number of foreclosures occurring on the East Coast were recorded, presaging the financial collapse of railroad stocks caused by rampant over-speculation. This led to the Panic of 1893, a period of widespread depression in the American economy, which had its hardships on Milwaukee Avenue.

Her painstaking search for relevant details was done by hand, as Google was still decades to come. The scrutiny of incremental lot-by-lot details became another fact base. In these days, Jeri noted, this class of common people kept no diaries, as many of them lacked basic handwriting skills, typical of their working-class Swedish and Norwegian culture. Her quantitative research was part of a new field of history scholarship. More importantly, Jeri's work embarked on the unprecedented field of common people's history. Their lives did not make them leaders of the corporate enterprises that shaped Minneapolis history, but their muscle and sweat made possible the production of the economic power for which the city had become known.

In the early 1970s, several older people on Milwaukee Avenue were as close as one generation away from the street's late nineteenth-century residents. Jeri interviewed several of these older people, whom she first met when she was door-knocking the neighborhood at the time of the University of Minnesota student antiwar strike. From these oral accounts, she learned the people's history of early Milwaukee Avenue. Jeri's paper contributed to the street's historic role in this period of American immigration. Minnesota Historical Society's Charlie Nelson saw its importance in the history of everyday people, and it became a highly important part of PAC's proposal to gain National Register status as a historic district.

Milwaukee Avenue's status as a historic district meant that a very lengthy federal process would be required to demolish any of the houses if their removal were to be contested. In addition, this National Register status intended to make local historic designation likely, which would give additional protection by requiring city-mandated building permit regulation for the appropriate architectural treatment of the houses. Milwaukee Avenue officially became a historic district on May 2, 1974, its placement signed by Secretary of the Interior Rogers C.B. Morton. The historic district boundaries included all residential properties facing Milwaukee Avenue but not the rest of the four-block area.

The most significant change in HRA operations was its recognition that the Milwaukee Avenue houses now became top rehab priorities. The question of what would be too few houses had vanished. Attendant to that, HRA assumed (wrongly) that historic designation had mandated demolition totally out of the question. (What designation did require was a careful examination at the federal level if PAC was to contest an HRA-proposed demolition.) HRA's main technical specialist, Tom Goodoien, applied his typical tenacious work habits to setting up methods to work with PAC to evaluate the houses. The planning team continued its work, now with full cooperation from various HRA staff members.

REHAB BECOMES REALITY

Several years before this time, many houses in Seward West, and especially on Twenty-second Avenue in the four-block area on Milwaukee Avenue, had gradually become rental properties. As such, their physical conditions deteriorated as they became occupied mostly by hippies and somewhat likeminded members of the counterculture. These were people bred with middle-class values who chose a volunteer, albeit selective, poverty that fit the times. During this era, certain music genres, like the blues, glorified people living on the edge with, as Bob Dylan put it, "no direction home... like a rolling stone." Now the newly owned HRA properties added more run-down houses to the immediate environs. The irony here was that houses no longer fit, for an older class of people who lived their lives with bare essentials had become an opportunity for a new younger class whose meager economic circumstances were eagerly elective.

That opportunity came at a fortuitous time for nearly everyone. By the time HRA had finally taken possession of many rental and owner-occupied houses, the agency had been bound by the aforementioned A and B lists. This meant that while A-list houses had been demolished according to prior agreement, B-list houses had been secured and boarded up right after the relocation of the former residents. At this time, another critical PAC-HRA program—rehabilitation—came into play. Now the counterculture had a "direction home" of sorts, becoming what the media eventually described as "urban pioneers." In Seward West, the term was "rehabbers."

The policy or directive that made rehabilitation operationally possible and had become the meta-principle for Seward West became reality only after the confluence of many circumstances. The bitter battle between PAC and HRA, in which rehab was the overarching issue, was decided without a ceremonious public declaration of the winner. The historic designation of Milwaukee Avenue could now be noted as the tipping point toward which both the strident PAC and the reluctant HRA had for some time been moving to put rehabilitation in place. Now HRA was mandated by federal authority to accept rehab and abandon a demolition-only policy for houses on Milwaukee Avenue, with enough factors in play that it could apply to houses outside of the historic district as well. In fact, the first houses to undergo rehab were not on Milwaukee Avenue but a few blocks away. Several factors opened up this possibility. The take-no-prisoners mentality of South Area director Jack Crimmins was replaced by that of his successors, who used measures of objectivity to determine rehab feasibility, which became a breakthrough. All this was pounded into place by PAC's incessant sledgehammer tactics.

More About Historic Designation

Milwaukee Avenue's placement on the National Register of Historic Places by the National Park Service in Washington, D.C., was a major accomplishment politically, but that status meant very little from a pragmatic viewpoint. The only real effect it had was that no federal money could be used to demolish a structure. The real regulatory mechanism was local designation, which required building permit approval to alter exteriors of a historic resource or approve its demolition. Designation would be critically important to prevent future maladroit changes to the exteriors of the houses. Our next move was application to the Minneapolis Heritage Preservation Commission (HPC) for local designation. We knew from past experience that HPC was ruled with a heavy hand by the Minneapolis Planning Department, which did not consider Milwaukee Avenue to merit local historic designation. But with the newly acquired federal historic listing, why would local authorities think otherwise? But HPC voted to deny historic designation. We were flabbergasted.

Asking a few people in the planning department to find out why this happened met with very polite disregard. Much later, in exploring HPC and planning commission meeting minutes for the research of this book, I discovered their rationale. A January 25, 1975 letter from planning department head Ralph W. Quiggle stated that the department did not consider Milwaukee Avenue worthy of historic designation. This letter was subsequently followed by an April 17 response from HPC chair Roy Thorshov, who wrote, "The Heritage Preservation Commission is not in agreement with the [planning] staff report with regard to the designation of Milwaukee Avenue." Thorshov followed with these points:

> *Milwaukee Avenue speaks to the experience of the working man, the laborer; there remains little legacy in Minneapolis of the life experience of this group in the early 20th century. That Milwaukee Avenue was shaped by the developer's desire for economic gain, at least what could be considered at the expense of the residents, is an aspect of our social history which this commission feels should not be denied.*[43]

However, an undated report by planning department staff put a bit of flavor in an otherwise bureaucratic prose. The report begins:

> *Any significance has been clouded in recent years by the forces of feelings against urban renewal. An Urban Renewal plan was written in 1960*

*which called for townhouses in this section of the Seward West Urban
Renewal Area. It is now fourteen years later, and that renewal plan still
exists but has not become a reality. Delays have been costly, and the housing
supply has decayed further. Sentiment has been aroused in support of this
type of housing that is not a historic sentiment. Reactions observed are
those tempered by feelings against the renewal of the area rather than for
preservation for historic, architectural or aesthetic reasons.*

The closing paragraph uses a pop-culture reference, misapplied for the
context at hand:

*Milwaukee Avenue is unique for its time simply for the number of cheaply
built housing units. It is a historical precursor to the tract housing of recent
origin described in a song of the early '60s as "little boxes made of ticky
tacky and they all look the same."*

When Tony Scallon heard of the planning department's intransigence, he
became angry, flew into action and brought his well-accrued political might
to bear where needed. Accordingly, HPC was ordered to put Milwaukee
Avenue's designation on its next public hearing agenda and to recommend
city council approval without hesitation. On July 25, 1975, the Minneapolis
City Council's resolution was approved, and Milwaukee Avenue was granted
designation as a local historic district.

Stan Fishman met several times with the PAC-HRA planning team to talk
about ideas for potential walkway and open-space planning. He established
a mutually shared design process. PAC staff members were a bit flattered
with his collaborative attitude, but they were later to discover that he had
long ago realized that time he spent drawing was time he couldn't spend
talking to people about what he would draw for them. The PAC conceptual
Milwaukee Avenue Four-Block-Area site plan, executed some time before,
became the basis for Fishman and Surendra's initial proposal, as it indicated
walkway and open-space design along with houses noted by addresses and
corresponding rehab cost estimates. PAC discovered that rehab estimates
for several addresses had incorrectly been changed from PAC evaluations,
but this was disregarded by PAC team members as the nature of this type
of preliminary planning process. As work on phase one continued, Stan
seemed to lack accuracy on specifics, but PAC staff was willing to overlook
it at the time, thinking they were making progress and that the study seemed
to reflect their hopes.

Similar to many other typical workman's cottages, 2009 Milwaukee Avenue had its original front porch rebuilt and enclosed.

By this time, the PAC planning team had developed a working method of transferring rehab component cost estimates established for previously identified cluster structures to function as a comparative base to those houses in other study clusters. Was this a valid way to find the necessary answers?

The architectural consultants readily agreed, and PAC's identified clusters appeared as houses for potential rehab on the preliminary development site plan—again with some incorrect addresses and rehab estimates. When informing them about the mix-up, the consultants gave assurance that the numbers still applied as shown on the plan. Hoping for hope, PAC team members went along with it.

Fishman and Ahuja's preliminary plan was received by the planning team with evenly balanced views. Jerri and the rest of the team stated that they felt the study was going in the right direction, although privately they were a bit apprehensive. The consultants treated the central issue of rehab feasibility with generalized rather than detailed attention, tending toward understatement.

At the time, PAC staff members were unaware that they had been thinking of the study process in terms much more complicated than had the consultants, which was why they thought the consultants should be fired. When they saw inaccuracies in the consultants' work and their limited understanding of core issues, they initially shrugged it off, with some underlying sense that perhaps these professionals with well-regarded reputations in planning and architecture should not be questioned by the likes of them. As the study continued in phase two, PAC team members began to incorporate their thoughts into their reports, which they passed along to Fishman and Ahuja. These reports were presented in the next planning team sessions at the HRA office, as were site plans mostly based on drawings John and I had prepared some time before. These successive drawings presented Fishman's flamboyant freehand style but were not developed with much more attention to design and planning on their part.

Part three of the planning work by Fishman and Ahuja was to provide marketing analysis. These real estate numbers were the necessary end-determinants for rehab feasibility. It was very important to know what the rehabbed houses would sell for at this time—even though HRA now felt committed to rehab and forced to accept whatever amount the houses would sell for. However, Fishman continued to perform his planning team presentations by much talking while waving his hands in the air. He told us at meeting after meeting that he would produce those figures, which he assured us was his most important work.

Eventually, the team's gradual apprehension of the Fishman-Ahuja planning effort turned into increasing dissatisfaction as the two planners became less and less productive. The PAC board expressed its frustration and hinted that the staff members were too allied with the consultants to

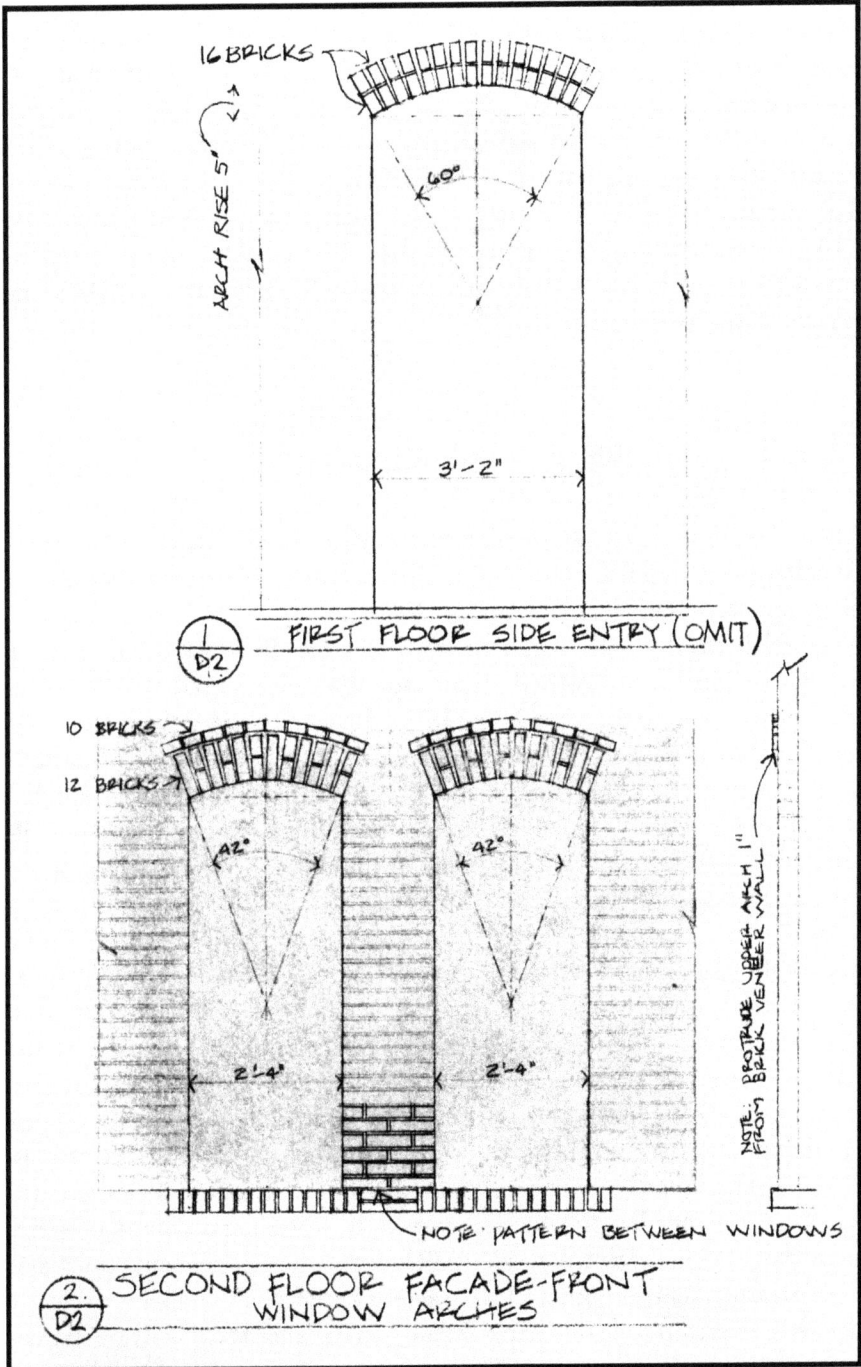

16 BRICKS

ARCH RISE 5"

60°

3'-2"

1
D2
FIRST FLOOR SIDE ENTRY (OMIT)

10 BRICKS

12 BRICKS

42°   42°

2'-4"   2'-4"

NOTE: PROTRUDE UPPER ARCH 1" FROM BRICK VENEER WALL

NOTE PATTERN BETWEEN WINDOWS

2
D2
SECOND FLOOR FACADE-FRONT WINDOW ARCHES

Architectural details developed by PAC staff members.

realize the situation for what it was. The hint was instructive, as was the strong suggestion that PAC staff confront them. We nervously did, and Fishman and Ahuja resigned.

Several PAC leaders met with the planning team to decide how to move forward. One evening, PAC planning staff met in Jeri's duplex unit, uneasy and unsure of what to do. When PAC leaders were asked who should be hired as replacements, the answer slowly but unmistakably became apparent. The leaders looked firmly at us but said no words. Then Jeri said, "We know exactly who can do it—we can."

WILLIAM RAGAN WAS A FUTURIST

The planning team spent considerable time on the here-and-now tasks of determining rehab feasibility, but an important objective was examining potential alternative forms of homeownership. The issue became whether the traditional form of homeownership, in which the house and the land it sits on are owned by an individual household and financed by a mortgage, could be adaptable to the complicated land issues in the four-block area. William Ragan's unique re-platting in the 1880s at first seemed problematic in view of the land's subsequently applied conventional zoning. The PAC team's planning for this six-and-a-half-acre area necessitated a means to own and control common areas interspersed with privately owned parcels.

In the early 1970s, condominium ownership was entering the housing picture. In large cleared land sites in the Twin Cities and the outer suburbs, owners purchased town houses, typically as part of a complex attached to other units. With mortgages tailored to this ownership, the land around the units was commonly owned by a homeowners association. The land was maintained and regulated by deed covenants stipulating use of various parts of common property and architectural controls on exterior alterations. A somewhat similar ownership, long used in very limited locations, was cooperative ownership, in which all parts of the dwelling units and property were owned equally by the residents. The proximity of dwelling units and their nearly identical physical characteristics strongly implies a clearly defined ownership code that can regulate and enhance the quality of shared-ownership living in this setting, defining the design character of building and spaces where many people live so near one another.

The Milwaukee Avenue Four-Block Area featured many of these characteristics with houses of consistent architecture close together that seemed to share town house attributes more than single property ownership, invoking the necessity to address how the issues of exterior alterations to building and property could affect the common community welfare. In this situation, HRA's eventual ownership of all houses facing Milwaukee Avenue and almost all of the properties within the four-block area now proved a more important site control mechanism, both for overall planning and to solve intricate and vexing problems of certain property line details' legal descriptions. PAC explored how a homeowners association could be formed and how this might manage the common issues that would arise with shared ownership of common spaces. After all, this was what PAC was all about—sharing responsibility to achieve something greater than itself.

The planning team studied a new residential zoning classification called planned unit development, or PUD (Minneapolis's version is called PRD), that allowed development projects to meet the overall zoning objectives when residential units were built in cluster arrangements within common areas. These developments would not have been possible with conventional zoning. PAC planners presented both the concept of condominium-style property ownership and PRD zoning at a regular PAC committee meeting. Considering the complications brought about by the common areas, it became apparent that traditional ownership could not work. But certain PAC members did not think that going completely condominium was appropriate.

The planning team had been consulting the legal staff at HRA for some time to ensure that PAC actions were appropriate. The team also met with the Minneapolis Planning Department, which had recently implemented PRD zoning. This was enthusiastically supported by Perry Thorvig and Bill Nordrum, the Young Turks of city planning at the time.

The city planning staff was very pleased with the team's concept and anxious to see PRD development take place in an area where conventional zoning would preclude situations in which creative approaches to development could occur. Up to this time, PRD zoning was applied exclusively to new town house developments. So the team asked Nordrum and Thorvig if the Milwaukee Avenue Four-Block Area, with its existing houses and the complications of a historic district, could meet PRD criteria. They enthusiastically said, "Let's try it!"

The primary aspect of community ownership was addressing a long-standing city zoning concern that the individually owned properties were very substandard in size (the city mandated a minimum lot size of four thousand square feet; some Milwaukee Avenue lots were little over half that size). Thorvig and Nordrum concluded that the open space of the right of way, if owned in "undivided interest" by a homeowners association, would satisfy the size requirement. Adding to the open space, a corner lot facing Milwaukee Avenue and East Twenty-second Street had been vacant for as long as anyone could remember—what better space for a mini-park with kids' play sculptures?

As a result, PAC was given the opportunity to have its cake and eat it, too. The houses and their properties would remain in traditional ownership, while the pedestrian walkway, mini park, group parking lots and other associated parcels of land intended for common use would be held in "undivided ownership." That common-use property would be held under title by the homeowners association, which would receive the deed covenants necessary to regulate and maintain the common areas. PRD became the framework through which multiple problems were solved. It allowed the significantly undersized lots to remain and be considered buildable if the existing house were lost to fire, in which case conventional zoning would not permit new replacement. It permitted, if not encouraged, the walkway and mini-park to be counted as sufficient open space related to each house, which many mortgage mechanisms required. It also permitted removal of the conventional street and gave vehicular access to individual houses on the east side of Milwaukee Avenue by using group parking lots

Houses on the east side of the Milwaukee Avenue walkway have parking access for residents in the form of five pocket parking lots, each holding seven cars. A narrow sidewalk situated between the backyards of these Milwaukee Avenue properties and houses along Twenty-third Avenue provide access to the lots.

A narrow walkway between the backyards of properties facing Milwaukee Avenue and Twenty-third Avenue connects households with nearby parking lots.

entered from Twenty-third Avenue. PRD requirements became a useful mechanism for community administration of its homeowners association and deed covenants. Its concept was simple, and the zoning was put in place in a short time. Later, however, legal steps necessary to establish deed covenants and its related aspects were excruciatingly difficult and threatened viability of the project.

In a broader context, PRD proved to be invaluable for historic preservation in that the historic district could not have continued to exist under the various inhibitions of underlying conventional zoning. Not until much later, thanks to a student paper written by Andrew Gibson for a historic preservation class at the University of Minnesota's School of Architecture, did we realize that William Ragan's speculative and innovative development in the 1880s, when he platted out 22½ Avenue and its diminutive residential lots, formed the makings of PRD nearly one hundred years later. In retrospect, Ragan seems so very prescient, considering re-platting the residential lots in 1976 altered only a few of these properties' lot lines by miniscule amounts. Moreover, his platting set out the remarkable rhythmic patterns composing the street's historic visual character, which PRD has preserved. Whatever was in his mind, William Ragan was an accidental futurist.

CHAPTER 13
Into the Thick of Planning

The public realm is what we own and control.
—*Michael Kimmelman,* New York Times, *December 4, 2011*

With Milwaukee Avenue no longer a city street, the City of Minneapolis would no longer own the right of way or conduct the maintenance, snow plowing and tree care that came with it. The obvious choice was for a homeowners association to take title and maintenance responsibility. A community-owned common space barring vehicle access drew forth another city requirement: parking space for each dwelling unit, especially those on the east side of Milwaukee Avenue with no front street or backyard automobile access. The houses on Milwaukee Avenue's west side shared an alley with Twenty-second Avenue houses (no problem here), but properties on the east side, with rear property lines abutting properties facing Twenty-third Avenue, would be "landlocked." The planning team came up with the idea to create a common sidewalk by borrowing a five-foot strip from the rear properties of the eastern Milwaukee Avenue houses and from the west boundary of those houses facing Twenty-third Avenue and running the north–south length of both blocks. By provident circumstance, the Twenty-third Avenue frontage had two long-existing vacant lots in the north block that could be converted into two common parking lots, each with seven parking spaces, providing auto access from Twenty-third Avenue. What could have been an eighth parking space could be converted to an enclosure for a trash container, with access for refuse trucks being provided by the parking lot and street. HRA had planned demolition of two small, crumbling Franklin Avenue commercial buildings on the corner of Franklin and Twenty-third Avenue that could provide enough space for remaining commercial storefronts and several residential spaces for the homeowners association. On the south block, outside the historic district, two conjoined lots were available due to a PAC-HRA agreed demolition of several severely deteriorated houses.

John and I drew many iterations of an overall detailed four-block area site plan containing the residential lots and the configuration of the aforementioned open spaces. Although the historic district boundaries included all residential properties facing Milwaukee Avenue (but not the rest of the four-block area), the four-block-area plan did not specifically demarcate the historic district's boundary lines, as the overall site treatment was seamless for all properties. When we thought we were ready, we presented our plan to Thorvig and Nordrum, and they were enthusiastic.

At every PAC meeting, we presented our progress, engendering much discussion regarding how parts of the plan could be tweaked. The ever so active PAC members and various involved people typically stopped in the PAC office several times between meetings, and I enjoyed showing them the latest plan aspects on which John and I had been working. These one-on-one chats provided a great opportunity for people

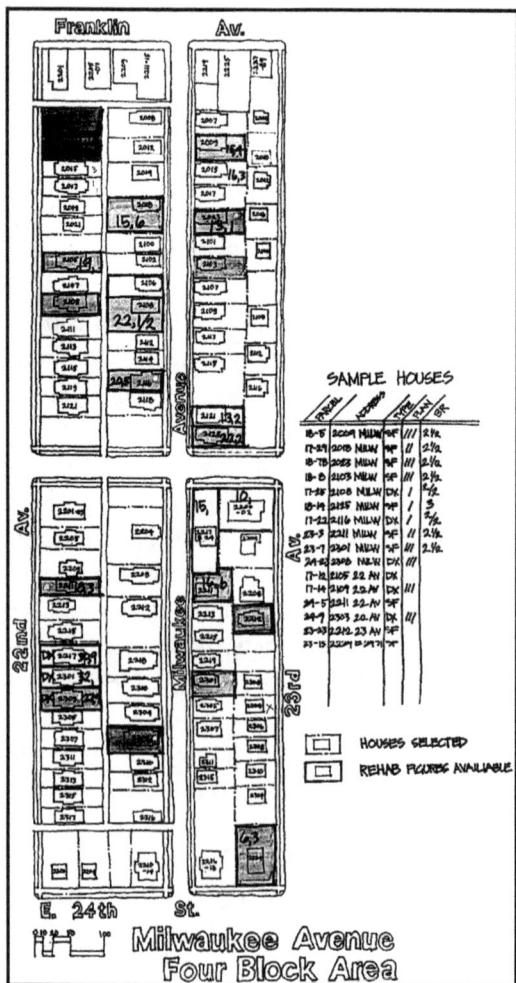

Above and next page: PAC staff members drew many versions of site plans.

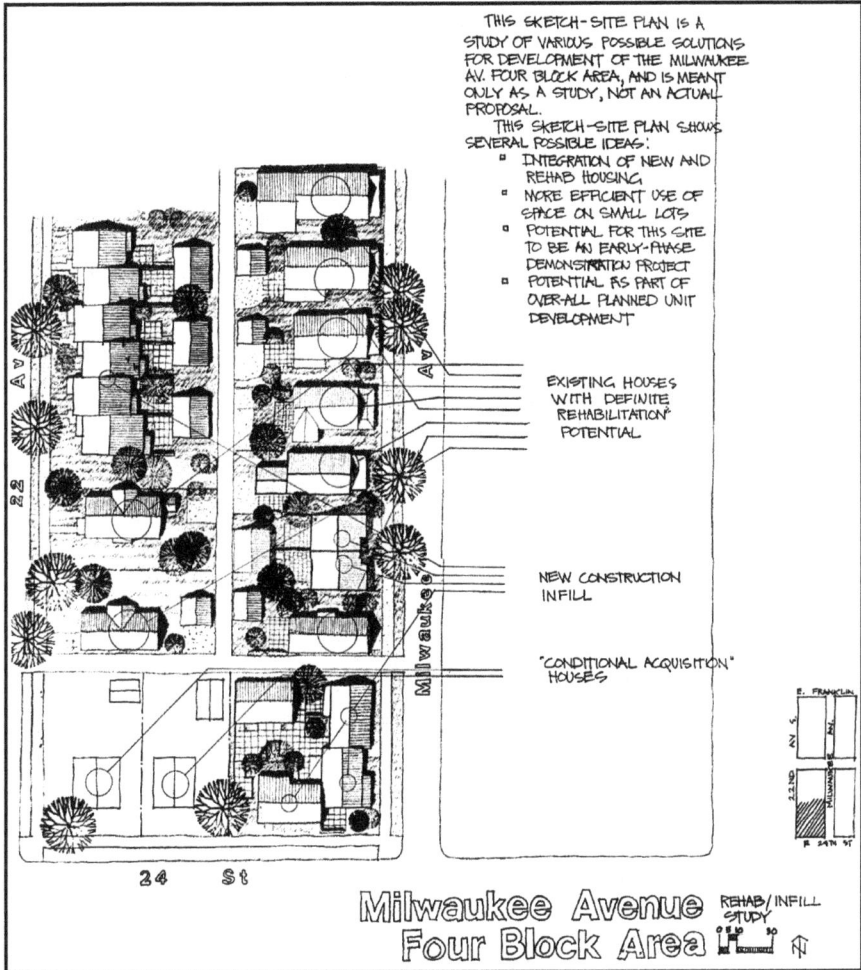

THIS SKETCH-SITE PLAN IS A STUDY OF VARIOUS POSSIBLE SOLUTIONS FOR DEVELOPMENT OF THE MILWAUKEE AV. FOUR BLOCK AREA, AND IS MEANT ONLY AS A STUDY, NOT AN ACTUAL PROPOSAL.
THIS SKETCH-SITE PLAN SHOWS SEVERAL POSSIBLE IDEAS:
- INTEGRATION OF NEW AND REHAB HOUSING
- MORE EFFICIENT USE OF SPACE ON SMALL LOTS
- POTENTIAL FOR THIS SITE TO BE AN EARLY-PHASE DEMONSTRATION PROJECT
- POTENTIAL AS PART OF OVER-ALL PLANNED UNIT DEVELOPMENT

EXISTING HOUSES WITH DEFINITE REHABILITATION POTENTIAL

NEW CONSTRUCTION INFILL

"CONDITIONAL ACQUISITION" HOUSES

Milwaukee Avenue REHAB/INFILL STUDY
Four Block Area

to understand the plan's complexities via these invaluable, exciting and highly informal back-and-forth sessions. Everybody could share in the design process.

Toward the final stages of site design, PAC members continued to support the four-block-area plan. However, as the gravity of the consequences mounted, the infighting between the organization's two opposing groups increased. Gradually, the differences became well defined. Some members and staff embraced the alternative thinking of the early 1970s and supported the plan as an innovative concept of houses and integrated common areas. Their long-standing opposition viewed the plan as unworkable and voiced support for traditional homeownership while keeping Milwaukee Avenue as a conventional street. The issue became heavily contentious. Tony, despite his

One of the final sketches used in designing the pedestrian walkway, street lighting and landscaping.

previous distrust of planning, had long been excited by our progressive plan and knew he had to ensure that an upcoming PAC meeting with this issue on the agenda would have a majority of supportive votes. Complicating the issue was the fact that one of the new PAC members involved in rehabbing a Milwaukee Avenue house voiced strong opposition to closing the street and having a homeowners association affecting his individual property rights. As the meeting and vote approached, the planning team members began to worry about the possible consequences. Voices of the opposition increased. When the PAC meeting took place and discussion of whether to approve the development plan ensued, I began to secretly count on my fingers the likely supporting votes. With my heart pounding, I listened to every nuance of each speaker, and after much contentious discussion, I realized, with some trepidation, that it would likely pass. PAC's vote to approve the plan passed by a four-vote margin.

In the plan's final design, I drew the open space to be a long, open semi-public space that included the walkways and boulevard-like grassy areas. John and Jeri added subtle ideas to make our design more pleasant and to allow the houses to make the most significant statement. We chose concrete as the paving material, consciously choosing a plain substance that would be consonant with a former working-class street. Nonetheless, we were occasionally asked why we didn't use cobblestones and whether there would be wrought-iron gates at both ends of Milwaukee Avenue. This would have been antithetical to the origins of the working-class historic district and would have given the place a history it never had.

Between porch faces on both sides of the open space, which varied from fifty to fifty-one feet, we designed long landscaped sections of primary open space. The paved walking path and grassy areas off-center of the open space became a modernist architectural precept, avoiding the formality of equilateral balance. The principal view emphasized the houses on the east face, benefitted by the verdant grassy surfaces as well as the trees planted in intervals. The paved pedestrian walkway, which required a fourteen-foot width for emergency vehicles, ran the west side of the open space and provided right-hand access via walking paths from Franklin Avenue. Also, the west side featured a majestic dominance of large and towering elm trees, which provided shade from afternoon sun.

Milwaukee Avenue's public space features a wide walkway that can accommodate emergency vehicles as well as pedestrian traffic.

Construction of the walkway began in 1976. Once the concrete had been poured and began to stiffen, concrete finishers scored lines that served as control joints and formed simple patterns suitable for the walkway's function.

John and I designed the grassy areas to be noticeably wider than the paved surfaces. The result was that the grassy areas and the walkway became subtly shaped by occasional three-foot offsets, allowing the paved areas to meander ever so slightly and giving more visual interest than would undeviating concrete paving. Near the center of the site, on the west side of the walkway, John designed the mini park. Along with imaginative sculptural play structures, it included a stepped-down sand space that gave a deft play of geometry to the park.

In February 1976, the four-block-area plan was complete, and PAC and HRA began the final review process. In a matter of months, Milwaukee Avenue would become the city's (and possibly the country's) first historic district with a landscape offering a pedestrian walkway on which residents could walk about and talk with their neighbors, children could ride their tricycles and chase one another and the general public could allow themselves to stray for a little while.

FINDING WAYS TO FINANCE REHAB

In the early 1970s in Washington, D.C., HUD developed programs to revitalize delivery of housing to the marketplace in ways that would address the increasing need for affordable housing. HUD's new system was called Community Development Block Grant (CDBG) funding.

DON'T LET THE MPLS. HOUSING AUTHORITY CAST A SHADOW OVER OUR NEIGHBORHOOD!

Support your Seward West Project Area Committee. They are fighting to save homes... not destroy them.

REMEMBER: Once "the man" downtown mutilates our neighborhood...it can never be replaced.

THINK REHAB!

AD HOC COMMITTEE TO PRESERVE, MAINTAIN, & REBUILD SEWARD WEST
721-2505

"Think Rehab!" This Seward West poster originated during the pre-PAC days when an ad hoc committee attempted to raise awareness of the negative effects of public agency renewal. Poster designed by Don Barton, photo by Roger Hankey.

The enactment of CDBG redirected certain funding to local governments—mayors and city councils—rather than public housing agencies. The mayor and city councils had more direct, albeit political, connection with communities, putting city lawmakers more in charge of renewal. This move was momentous for community groups, many of which were setting up nonprofit housing organizations and forming relationships with city government. This put decision-making for neighborhood development more in this city-neighborhood nexus, with housing authorities becoming administrative functionaries.[44] Another important benefit was putting more certainty in the redevelopment process, especially for active neighborhoods' ability to use public funding.

In Minneapolis, the newly elected mayor, Al Hofstede, became the city's first policy wonk. In 1974, his administration crafted a number of programs, some of which could interlock together, offering defined subsidies to development projects where urban conditions would otherwise fail to meet an accountant's bottom line. Housing was a prime beneficiary of subsidy in urban renewal areas, where lower house values inhibited the profit margin by builders. Among the Hofstede administration's new housing policies, administered by HRA, were two components that took place in Seward West: (1) rehab targeted toward owner-occupied properties could receive an $8,000 grant if the owner occupied the house for a minimum of five years, and (2) the individual rehab program offered homeowners an 8 percent combined construction loan (the going rate at the time was 16 percent) and mortgage, likewise specifying an owner-occupancy period.

The most critical part of the new policy was called "rehab write-down." The gap measured in dollars between the cost of rehab and land purchase, when exceeding sales costs for nonprofit developers, became the dollar amount, or write-down, for HRA to provide the funding to close the gap. For example, if a house's rehab costs and land costs (which HRA often lowered to $1) totaled $40,000 and the real estate market value was $31,000, the rehab write-down amount was $9,000.

CDBG came at the right time for Seward West and Milwaukee Avenue. In the pre-CDBG years, HRA held an upper hand in debates on rehab feasibility with PAC, insisting on a formula that a house's rehab costs plus land costs could not exceed 75 percent of its market price. Even with low estimated rehab costs, the result would have saved fewer houses. Mayor Hofstede's rehab write-down program essentially subsidized rehab, a critical factor in maintaining the traditional identity of urban neighborhoods. According to Patricia Mack, Hofstede knew how to "max" the largesse of CDBG. In Seward West, these newly instituted subsidy programs carried a certain irony in that they were limited to house rehab and not applicable to new construction, which HRA originally counted on to rebuild Seward West.

THE MILWAUKEE AVENUE COMMUNITY CORPORATION

In mid-1974, Tony Scallon and a few PAC leaders were well aware that they had scored an important step in saving Milwaukee Avenue, but only as a policy in the whole realm of city government workings. Now they needed to take the next step toward initiating the rehab process. What they didn't realize was that they were about to save Milwaukee Avenue by not making a profit.

Thus far in the Twin Cities and in many other areas of the nation, the small groups undertaking these types of rehab processes had no real models or precedents to follow, resulting in the groups inventing what they thought was needed and applying whatever expertise they could muster. In many areas, various groups found themselves unable to fulfill the destiny of their much-wrought transcendent aspirations of rehabilitating houses. They infused themselves with all the idealism that PAC worked with but none of the pragmatic foundation had held it up straight. If anything, many PAC members felt uneasy with idealism.

Seward West Redesign, the neighborhood-organized nonprofit housing organization, began in 1970 with well-balanced earnestness and purpose. But a few years later, most of the leadership of this group had begun strongly emphasizing radical ideology directed toward vehement attacks against city government, HRA in particular. Housing development was far less important. Redesign caused a political rift in PAC, as some members thought it expedient, if not exciting, to have an outside community contingent embarrass local government. While some members viewed radicalism as an important means to bring about change, radicalism here was misplaced and unrealistic—an impediment to redirecting HRA Seward West policy and forming much-needed new policies. The ideology split within PAC remained a background issue, but when Milwaukee Avenue development became a possibility, members organized a nonprofit housing organization dedicated to rehabilitating selected houses in the four-block area. The organization became known as the Milwaukee Avenue Community Corporation (MACC).

The four-block-area rehabilitation was implemented via funds from two principal sources: the MACC and the City of Minneapolis's Individual Rehab Program. MACC assembled its financing package with funding supplied by the Greater Minneapolis Metropolitan Housing Corporation (GMMHC) and the Catholic Archdiocese of St. Paul.

CHAPTER 14

Rehab Begins

During the years it took to prove Milwaukee Avenue was worth saving, Jeri would say that the politics and bureaucracy were more difficult than the actual rehab could ever be. I wasn't so sure. I had worked as a laborer on building construction during four summers while in college and for a year between my first and second years of architecture school and knew well the physical stamina it took to get through the workday. But when the politics and bureaucracy at last yielded to hammers and lumber, I acknowledged Jeri's observation.

The architectural drawings prepared by John Wicks and myself received assistance from architectural students in the Minneapolis Community Design Center. Two of the houses in MACC's first rehab package, 2009 and 2107 Milwaukee Avenue, were located on the east side of Milwaukee Avenue just south of Franklin, where the visual impact of the street's revitalization would be most evident. Two other houses were located on Twenty-second Avenue South, outside the historic district, as redevelopment included the overall four-block area. Ron Soderberg Construction, a St. Paul contractor with considerable rehab experience, was awarded the contract. Jeri, John and I eagerly awaited Ron's carpentry crew to begin work, but his company was having a busy work schedule, so we somehow learned to be patient.

The launch for rehab on the first Milwaukee Avenue house came in mid-1975, when PAC and MACC sponsored a kickoff event. To counter the trite shovel-in-the-ground groundbreaking ceremony, we held an "un-boarding ceremony." We secured a few crowbars, sprayed them with gold

An architectural rendering intended to portray the eventual rehabilitation of Milwaukee Avenue.

paint and organized a press event. The media stood in full force in front of 2009 Milwaukee Avenue's boarded-up front porch as mayor Al Hofstede council members Tom Johnson and Zollie Green and GHMMC director Chuck Krusell spoke. This was followed by the mayor wielding the gold-painted crowbar to pull off one of the plywood panels, symbolizing the start of Milwaukee Avenue rehabilitation.

On a cold December morning in 1975, the next battle in the war to save Milwaukee Avenue began. Soderberg Construction started gutting the innards of 2108 Milwaukee Avenue, the first of five houses in our rehab package, which also included 2009 Milwaukee, 2107 Milwaukee, 2107 Twenty-second Avenue South and 2009 Twenty-second Avenue South.

MACC sponsored the rehab of fourteen houses—eleven on Milwaukee Avenue and three on Twenty-second Avenue. MACC's presence helped catalyze rehabilitation in the four-block area. The construction cost for 2009 Milwaukee Avenue was approximately $41,000, and the property's sale price was $30,700. The difference between those figures, $10,300, was the rehab

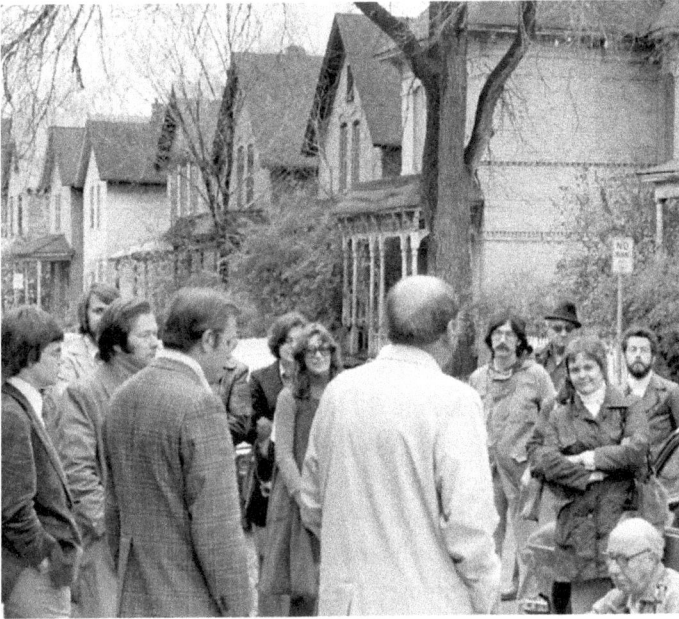

This photo was taken at the "un-boarding" ceremony hosted by the Milwaukee Avenue Community Corporation, a nonprofit housing organization sponsored by PAC. The official kickoff for the rehab process was attended by the mayor of Minneapolis and other city officials, who used "gold" crowbars to pry off the plywood panels covering the deteriorated porch window openings.

The Soderberg carpentry crew takes a lunch break on the porch of a Milwaukee Avenue house.

141

write-down number. In this first house package, similar write-down amounts were incurred by the four other properties. But rehab write-downs decreased as MACC's work prompted increased market value of the rehabilitated houses. Much public attention came through newspaper articles and television news stories. Shortly after MACC's houses were underway, the individual rehab program was at work on other houses along the street and throughout Seward West.

REHAB'S FIRST STEPS

House rehab began in various parts of Seward West shortly before it began on Milwaukee Avenue. In the following years, the sound of power saws and the pounding of hammers could be heard all over the neighborhood. Where lots were cleared of irreparable houses, new framing lumber on fresh concrete-block foundations began to appear. PAC and HRA were busy planning land sales as rehab-ready houses and buildable lots became available. PAC handled the buyers selection process, and HRA administered the financial paperwork. Staff of both organizations met almost daily to coordinate the growing number of properties ready for the market.

The rehab process often began with building new full-depth foundations for basements. The houses' interiors were completely gutted of all lath and plaster, interior trim, plumbing, electrical lines and fixtures, space heaters, chimneys and other miscellaneous debris that remained behind. Interiors became bare skeletons of interior partitions and wall framing. The hardwood floors were still usable despite having endured decades of the families who had tread on them, and similarly, the stairs and their lathe-turned balusters (spindles) and newel posts were generally fit to serve new lives in the soon-to-be renovated houses. On the exterior, the derelict porches were easily ripped down. A seemingly monumental task was removing the brick from the house sheathing. These larger expanses of original brick, unstable after years of settling and cracking, could not be economically repaired. Brick veneer was removed by workers using pipes from old clothes-line poles and hauled away to a brickyard in a North Minneapolis industrial area where large piles of brick from demolished industrial buildings awaited removal of remaining mortar. The cleaned brick was then stacked in pallets to be recycled for various construction purposes, some probably supplied back to Milwaukee Avenue.

This page: Before-and-after shots taken during the gutting of a typical workman's cottage. The interiors of the houses were gutted of lath and plaster, deteriorated wood trim, floor coverings, plumbing and electrical systems, space heaters and miscellaneous items. The exterior brick was typically too deteriorated to repair, so it was removed and later replaced with reusable brick of the same color and texture. The replacement bricks came from scores of demolished warehouse buildings near downtown areas.

143

After the houses were gutted, they were lifted onto steel beams laid across wood cribbing. The purpose was to lift the structure high enough for the excavation of new basements.

A bulldozer excavates a new basement underneath the beam-supported structure. Concrete footings were poured, followed by the building of concrete-block foundation walls. When the mortar was set, the house was lowered onto the new foundation.

Once the structure was ready, the contractor hired Doepke Building Movers to raise the house up off its old crumbling limestone foundation. The structure was perched on long steel beams resting on wood cribbing, high enough for a bulldozer to crawl underneath to excavate enough earth for a full-depth basement. Concrete footings were poured, and a concrete-block foundation was built. When the mortar of the concrete work was cured, the house was lowered onto the new foundation, and the process of rehabilitation could now begin.

ESTABLISHING MILWAUKEE AVENUE HISTORIC PRESERVATION STANDARDS

The first rehab package put into brick and mortar what PAC architectural staff had developed on the drawing board to be the preservation rehab standards for these recently designated historic houses. We were guided by Charlie Nelson, historic architect for the State Historic Preservation Office, who operated in a very informal manner and with innate kindness in providing us with the appropriate federal guidelines affecting our design methodology. What this meant was that exteriors were subject to the preservation of original architectural features, while the interiors were not affected by the guidelines. We made no changes to the components of the exterior envelope, but due to extreme deterioration and missing materials, we replaced original elements with new material cut and shaped to original design and retained exact locations and configurations of window and door openings. Historic preservation prior to this time focused on careful restoration, meaning specific treatment to preserve all original materials of prominent high-style buildings.

Houses on Milwaukee Avenue were subject to historic preservation guidelines that affected exteriors only, with most attention focused on front façades facing the street. At first, the guidelines were generally worded, stating that window openings be kept in their original sizes and locations. Maintaining the exact roof pitches, which critically affected the remarkable rhythm of the houses, was also spelled out. Porches were required to be open and to respect the historical profiles, with no specified language to replicate original details.

Milwaukee Avenue houses were vernacular structures with significant deterioration and had been built as rudimentary shelters. Foundations were built with low-grade limestone extending not much more than

The exterior of 2100 Milwaukee Avenue was restored to original. The interior was transformed into a more contemporary space.

a foot into the ground, with not even enough room for crawlspaces. Exterior ornamentation was limited to porches and triangular gable panels. Interiors were basic, with no dining room cabinets and kitchens furnished only for rudimentary functions. There were also extreme considerations—front porches had become severely deteriorated, many having been closed in with makeshift windows, and all but a few houses' brick walls had been covered with stucco, probably attempts to stabilize large cracks in the façade.

So many of these conditions made restoration, the modus operandi of historic preservation, inoperative and rehabilitation—retaining original materials where possible and using new compatible replacement materials—imperative. Rehabilitation is typically defined as retaining basic components, repairing existing material where feasible and replacing materials too deteriorated to repair with new or reused compatible materials. In the case of these Milwaukee Avenue houses, new replacement reached considerable magnitude. Our drawings included new basements that would rid the houses of the spooky, decrepit crawlspaces. They also delineated exact replication for new porches based on the original workman's cottage design. The same held for rear

This image of the front porch at 2015 Milwaukee Avenue displays the attention to detail performed during the house's 1976 rehabilitation. At that time, the existing porch, decrepit and badly altered from its original state, was removed. Lathe-turned columns were formed from drawn templates made from a neighbor's porch, as were the scroll-cut ornamental spandrels and the rows of lathe-turned spindles above. The original front door was repaired for reuse, and the new top door trim shows a scroll-cut pattern reproduced from an original design found on nearby doorways.

porches. One house on the street had retained its original front porch, complete with ornamental details. John measured the porch's features and drew templates for ornamental spindle friezes, spandrels and lathe-turned columns. Other commonly occurring details, including interior trim, were included in the architectural documents to be replicated with new wood at a millwork shop. PAC staff passed the detail sheets along to individual rehabbers.

2018 Milwaukee Avenue was one of the first completed rehab houses.

MACC had tight budgets with which to work, tightening the rehab write-down amount available from city financial sources. The initial rehab cost estimates came in high, so we had to look for ways in which we could bring down costs without reducing historical appropriateness. Some revisions, such as porch footings, minor interior trim details and reduced lighting fixtures allowances, could be made without altering the architecture. This was expressed to the general contractor in language that clarified the details and procedures.

When these houses were originally built, plaster was the only material available for interior walls, but the pre–World War II introduction of sheetrock revolutionized interiors for all buildings. Sheetrock was much easier and cheaper to install, and its hardened paper surface readily took on paint and was much smoother than plaster. As a result, sheetrock trumped plaster for Milwaukee Avenue houses, as the cost of plaster was three to four times that of sheetrock.

Window sash on the original houses featured shallow arched tops. These were very costly to manufacture, however, and a compromise became necessary. Flat sash were substituted, while the brick arches enclosing the tops of the window frames were maintained. It was a slightly noticeable but very minor change to the exterior architecture. These revised changes made the budget work. We kept less obvious elements such as tongue-and-groove porch ceilings and slightly wider but authentic wood trim for exterior doors and windows.

There were no historic preservation guidelines applicable to interior design. The original front part of the floor plan of the typical houses had small parlors, or living rooms, flanked on one side by a hallway and the main stairway. A large dining room with a narrow mother-in-law bedroom on one side occupied the house's middle section, joined by a sizeable kitchen and accompanying enclosed reach porch. Original kitchens usually consisted of a wall-mounted sink, a stove, a refrigerator and a short section of enameled steel cabinets with a pullout countertop. The second floor held two bedrooms and a bathroom.

For the most part, the floor plans stayed true to the originals. This helped MACC meet the tight budget it had for the first five houses. The bathrooms were updated with ceramic tile on the floors and some of the walls. Kitchen layouts provided continuous countertops integrating sinks and stoves, introducing this postwar feature to Milwaukee Avenue houses for the first time. Most of the rehabilitation concentrated on basic improvements such as new sheetrock, plumbing, heating and electrical

The workman's cottage at 2009 Milwaukee Avenue was one of the first rehab houses completed in 1976.

systems, doors and trim. Exterior restoration included building new basements, replacing brick walls, installing new windows and doors, replacing roofs and adding new porches. In the next two phases, first-floor walls, formerly those of the front hallway, dining room and mother-in-

150

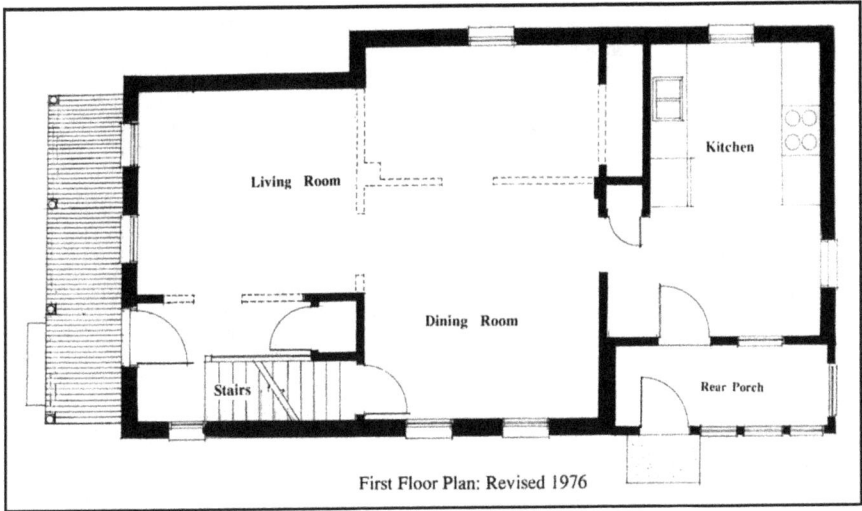

First Floor Plan: Revised 1976

This first-floor plan, created for the 1976 rehab, depicts revisions to the original workman's cottage plan.

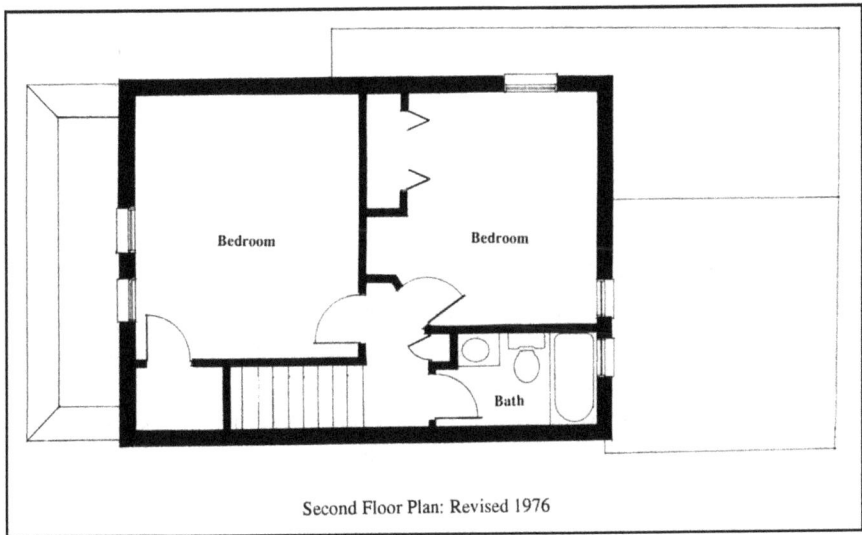

Second Floor Plan: Revised 1976

The second-floor plan for the 1976 rehabilitation. Bathrooms were added to Milwaukee Avenue houses after outdoor plumbing became antiquated.

law bedroom, were removed in order to enlarge the former dining room. This transformation created one commodious space out of four rooms, allowing more flexible use within a tight architectural envelope.

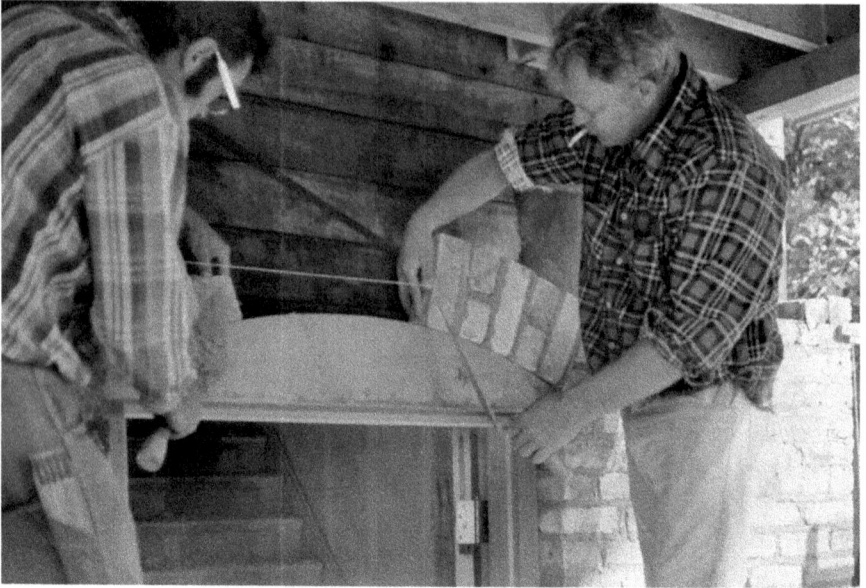

Bricklayers constructing the arch over a doorway. An arched wooden form was set in to the masonry opening, and the bricklayers laid the brick in place. Once the mortar had set, the form was removed.

BRICKWORK

The brick that veneers the Milwaukee Avenue houses produces a sense of aesthetic solidity that only it can provide. Brick walls were built with a single width, or "wythe," laid in courses and anchored to exterior wall sheathing with corrugated galvanized metal anchors nailed every two feet in vertical and horizontal locations. Mortar was selected to match the original in both color and texture. At window and door openings, the bricklayers used slightly curved wooden forms to set the brick in arched configurations above the open space. After a few days, when the mortar had dried, the forms were removed. With the mortar dried, the bricklayers washed the surfaces with water and a soft solution to clean away tiny leftover mortar crumbs, and the brickwork was complete.

CHAPTER 15

The Individual Rehab Program (If You Had a Hammer)

The Individual Rehab Program (IRP), a program encompassing the entire Seward West Urban Renewal Area, began in the four-block area shortly before MACC's rehab began and completed its last house in the mid-1980s. Rehabbers could perform all carpentry work, but roofing, excavation and foundation work were typically performed by general contractors. Plumbing and heating was to be performed by licensed contractors; electrical work required a licensed contractor to install the meter and electrical panel, but a homeowner could install the circuits, receptacles and fixtures that had to meet various levels of inspections. An important part of the redevelopment contract required submission of specifications that spelled out technical details for more extensive rehabilitation standards in addition to those stipulated by the building code.

To be eligible for the rehab program, the applicant first met with PAC staff for general orientation and to receive information about particular houses available. PAC staff would give the applicant basic information about income requirements, acquire a general assessment regarding his or her experience and familiarity with skills necessary to do the work and give information on how to work with various subcontractors. The applicant then met HRA staff to begin the financial application process.

Almost all of the people involved with the IRP program were in their twenties or thirties, and a few were in their early forties. Occupational backgrounds varied. There were professionals, teachers, officeworkers

A pair of friends rehabilitated adjacent houses on Milwaukee Avenue.

and other entry-level workers with meager incomes. They were typically couples (some married, some not), while others were single men and women. With most couples, women worked full time to provide the main source of income and the out-of-pocket expenses while the men worked on the houses. The men managed to interrupt their jobs for several months or worked part time so they could concentrate on their carpentry, becoming househusbands under an extended definition of that term. Women spent evenings and weekends participating in the rehab work. In these early days of the women's movement, many women found learning to work with hammers, saws and drills an attractive skill.

PLASTER DUST GETS IN YOUR EYES

Rehabilitating the houses began once all the government paperwork had been placed in the correct files (although it sometimes surreptitiously started before that) and the building permit issued. The HRA padlock was removed from the front door, and the rehabbers and volunteer gutting crew took over. The crew donned facemasks covering noses and mouths and began wielding crowbars to tear away lath and plaster from walls and ceilings, along with unusable wood trim. Debris quickly covered the floors, and a grayish cloud of plaster dust soon filled the air. Some of that dust could affect the eyes, and more than a few people came back with goggles for their second stints. The typical gutting process involved crew members taking turns pulling down lath and plaster and using big scoop shovels to toss the debris out window openings and into the dumpster.

Typically, the gutting crew consisted of other rehabbers who joined together to get a time-consuming and task-specific job done expeditiously. A four- to five-person gutting crew, depending on variable conditions, could get all or most of the interior gutting done in a weekend, with a number of volunteers contributing shifts of several hours.

Most homeowners decided to remove all lath and plaster and accompanying wood trim. One reason was that the considerable number of plaster surfaces, which had accumulated numerous cracks and fallen-out areas during many years of existence, would have required many hours of skilled repair. The plastering trade at that time had nearly disappeared from construction practice. Much of the plaster in these nearly century-old houses was in such a precarious state that beginning a repair job would often loosen adjacent areas, causing large sections of necessary replacement. New interior design meant that many interior partition walls would be removed to create new spaces. More important, bare, studded walls at interior faces of exterior walls and exposed bottoms of floor joists made installation of electrical wiring, plumbing lines and heating ductwork easier than if installed by "fishing" lines and wires through concealed conditions covered by plaster. Also, open framing offered the ability to more easily apply insulation batting and sheets of vapor barrier to exterior walls and ceiling areas, which would provide a more effective insulated envelope and reduce heating costs. An additional factor was the relative ease with which sheetrock walls and ceilings could be installed.

Exterior sheathing and all or most of the siding remained, depending on condition. Roof rafters and sheathing also remained in place, subject to isolated repair, and roof shingles were almost always replaced due to weathering. Windows, also affected by weather adversities, and doors, both exterior and interior, were also replaced. Floor joists, subfloor boards and top-layer hardwood flooring were usually sound enough to be retained and repaired. Stairway steps and supporting structure, if the

Carpenters reframing the roof of a cottage on Milwaukee Avenue. For most homes, the original rafters and sheathing were able to be reused during the rehab process by adding a layer of plywood.

new floor plan kept them in place, were almost always stout enough to continue service despite their years of use; the top members of railings sometimes could be reused, as could their balusters (spindles). More often than not, wood trim surrounding door openings and window frames were removed due to their often scarred, cracked or mismatched conditions.

SLAMMING HAMMERS: MEASURING TWICE AND CUTTING ONCE

The slamming of hammers and the whine of power saws signaled the beginning of rough carpentry, which essentially revised existing interior framing. If necessary, new door and window openings were built, as were wall partitions for rooms and closets, undergirding for new stairways and other framing or finish surfaces.

This photograph, taken in the mid-1970s, shows that various rehab work was well underway on several houses on Milwaukee Avenue.

FINISH CARPENTRY

After sheetrock was installed, taped and sanded, a primer coat and a finishing coat of paint were applied. Trim members were then installed. This begins the finish carpentry phase, in which the work becomes more exact and carefully applied. The pace of construction slowed significantly. Saw cuts were more precisely measured, according to the carpenter's maxim: "Measure twice and cut once." Nailing trim members in place required considerably more skill and time than rough carpentry, as abutting or mitered surfaces had to fit tightly together with no perceptible room for error. Installing reconditioned existing trim required even more skill and much more time and patience. In most situations, all of the trim installed was new material. Most houses' existing or original trim members required considerable labor to refinish them, even though many rehabbers liked the "character" of old wood.

As the project approached the finishing stage, ceramic tile, kitchen cabinets and countertops were installed, followed by kitchen floor coverings and sanding and applying polyurethane to hardwood floors. For many houses in the Individual Rehab Program, the owners were allowed to move in and assume temporary occupancy. While they settled into their rehabilitated home, exterior repair and replacement could be done at a more relaxed pace.

In late weekday afternoons, several rehabbers would occasionally leave work early—and up and down Milwaukee Avenue, one could hear the sounds of hammers and power saws. One would often see a yellow power cord leading from one house to another, where a rehabber with a live power panel would be lending electricity to his neighbor until he had his panel installed. Soon, a rehabber would be talking with another rehabber or two about daily progress and difficulties to be overcome. And if the occasion were right, the visiting rehabber would lend a hand, combining socializing with helping out.

An unforeseen benefit of the IRP was the intense camaraderie that it produced. People shared how-to tips, tools, food, beer and wine. Given the great number of houses undergoing rehab, various peer groups throughout the area quickly formed to set up informal cooperative learning sessions, which increased skill levels in many rehabbers. Some Friday afternoons, a six-pack or two would show up on somebody's sawhorses at a jobsite, and a relaxing moment would occur. Seward West became home to the urban version of a barn-raising event, where many hands gathered for gutting, framing, hanging sheetrock and painting.

Carpentry work being performed on a Milwaukee Avenue porch during rehabilitation.

By August 1976, many more houses on Milwaukee Avenue were in the rehab process; four had been completed, and twelve were being readied for work.

DEFINING THE ARCHITECTURE FOR REHAB

For the most part, homeowners in the IRP in other areas throughout Seward West conserved the traditional architectural character on their houses' exteriors, making minor alterations that stayed within the original design. Several houses in the four-block area became interesting examples of architectural designers who followed all the historic preservation rules regarding the exteriors while adding their own touches to the interiors. Steve Jensen at 2012 Milwaukee Avenue, Harold Fournier at 2204 Milwaukee Avenue and Charlie Anderson at 2201 Twenty-second Avenue each spent

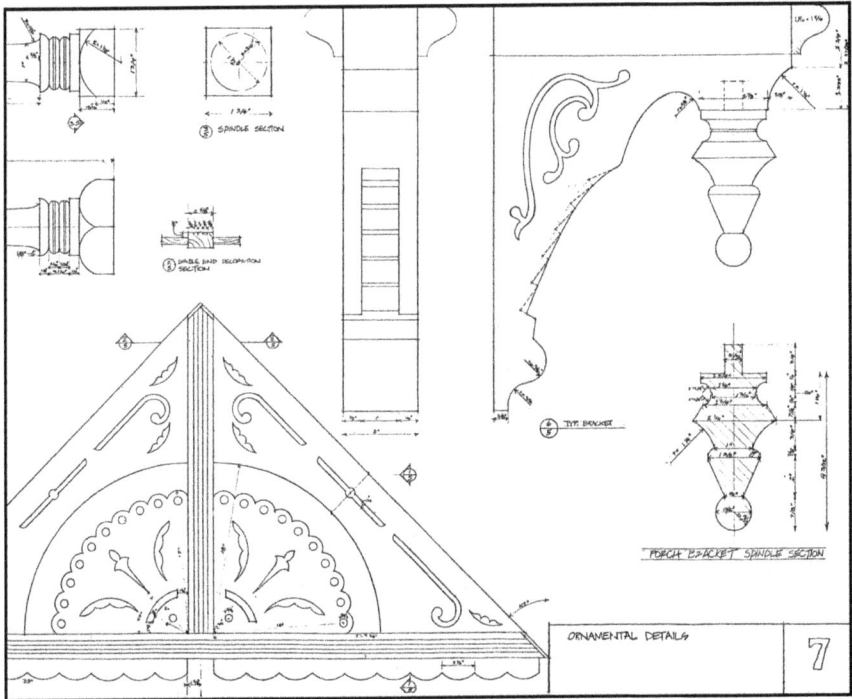

Architectural details used for the rehab of porches and other elements on Milwaukee Avenue houses.

A former fourplex at the south end of Milwaukee Avenue originally had its main entry facing East Twenty-fourth Street. In the early 1980s, the severely dilapidated structure was transformed into three side-by-side town houses, with an added front porch and entrances facing Milwaukee Avenue.

a year or so at the University of Minnesota School of Architecture and then left to become carpenters. When Milwaukee Avenue houses became available for the IRP, they took advantage of the opportunity to combine their recently acquired architectural design knowledge with their developing carpentry skills.

Jensen, Fournier and Anderson designed interiors in abstract geometries that paired minimalism with complexity. Likewise, these minimalist spaces contradicted what was occurring with restoring the houses' historically articulated exterior shells. Modern architecture became appropriately melded with historicism.

At the south end of Milwaukee Avenue was an extremely dilapidated fourplex. The side-by-side units on both levels had shotgun-type floor layouts running the length of the building, with the main entrances and stairways at the south façade facing East Twenty-fourth Street. These floor layouts were totally revised by designing two vertical transverse party walls, which formed three adjacent town house–type units. Each unit's front door faced Milwaukee Avenue, sheltered by a new porch that transformed what had been the side of the building into its main façade.

CHAPTER 16

Harold and Connie Fournier

Today, Harold and Connie Fournier seem relaxed and content. Their rehab at 2204 Milwaukee Avenue represents the epitome of the 1970s historic preservation house rescue: a faithful obedience to exterior restoration, with the inside spaces having been removed of room-defining partition walls to create modern architectural three dimensionality and spatial configurations accommodating new living patterns. On Milwaukee Avenue, the Fourniers became the embodiment of that quote by Winston Churchill that many architects love to repeat: "We shape our buildings; thereafter they shape us." For Harold and Connie, there is a double meaning. The architecture they created at 2204 defined not only how their sensibilities affected and were affected by their dwelling but also their ensuing professional lives; Connie later became deputy director of Minneapolis Department of Building Inspections, and Harold began work as a carpenter for Kraus Anderson Construction Companies (later becoming a superintendent for multimillion-dollar building projects).

For the Fourniers, Churchill's word "shape" works better as "reshape." The pair began their house rehab in 1977 by pulling away veneer brick from the exterior. They discovered that the wood framing at the house's rear section was too rotted to drive nails into, so they tore it off and reconstructed over half of the house's original framing.

More than a year earlier, in 1976, the newlyweds had moved from their hometown of Duluth to Minneapolis, where Connie began her public agency career and Harold entered the School of Architecture at the University of

Minnesota. A year later, their cramped, cheap apartment unit had become unbearable, so Connie and Harold had to take action. Both Harold and Connie grew up with carpenter fathers who built the houses in which they lived. Each of them had helped their fathers and knew a few things about building houses. So it was somehow in their blood to be collaborative builders of their own shelter. But how could they build their own house when they didn't have any money?

At that time, only Connie had a job. Harold had just finished his first year in architecture school, which he decided was his last one. He found occasional work doing carpentry. But the desire to build their own home grew strong, and Harold began to drive his Volkswagen Beetle around the city to look for condemned houses. One day he happened to glance down Milwaukee Avenue, which was lined with what looked to Harold like many shabby vacant houses. He stopped his Volkswagen in front of a vacant structure at 2204 Milwaukee, looked at it and then wrote its address in his notebook, followed by the words "a lost cause."

But Harold sensed a certain spirit in this street. He talked to a few people working on a house rehab and asked how he could find out how to buy one of the empty houses. A few minutes later, Harold was in the Seward West PAC office meeting with Jeri Reilly, who explained the Seward West PAC lottery system. Each of the available vacant HRA-owned houses had multiple applicants, and the next lottery was over a month away. Harold mentioned to Jeri that if he weren't selected, he would have to wait and again take a chance to wait for the next one. Jeri told him that there was one house available that nobody had applied for in the last few events and that if he were interested, he could be selected as the applicant right away—pending a credit and income report. Harold asked the address, and Jeri responded, "It's 2204 Milwaukee."

The Fourniers decided this was their only option to have their own house. When they asked Jeri how much income they needed to qualify, Jeri told them that they need some income but not too much because they had to fit into a low-income category. Eventually, the Fourniers qualified for a $15,000 city loan at 8 percent, a federal Section 312 loan for $15,000 at 2 percent and a Minnesota Historical Society grant of $6,000. On July 7, 1977, their paperwork was ready to be finalized for their redevelopment agreement. An HRA land sales officer told Harold and Connie that they needed to write a check for a specified percentage of the existing land value, which was $108. Connie thought hard about this—she knew public agencies typically did not cash checks a day after receiving them, but if HRA cashed her check the next day, their account balance would not cover it. Payday would come two days later. Connie handed over her check, hoping for the best. This event changed their lives.

Here the story needs a temporary fast forward: more than five months later, on December 20, with their rehab well underway, Connie received a letter from HRA stating that the accounting department had somehow lost her $108 check and requesting that she resubmit that amount to them.

Harold unlocked the HRA padlock and went to work with his crowbar, jerking away lath and plaster. He scooped up debris and threw it in a dumpster outside a window opening. It didn't take long with neighbors sharing tools, newly discovered rehab techniques and parts of houses such as newel posts, trim pieces and claw-foot bathtubs. Somebody's wheelbarrow became a community materials transport vehicle. Somebody's well-worn pickup truck could be borrowed for trips to the lumberyard. Their carpentry, the building materials they used and their home-grown barter system made them self-assigned outcasts of the conventional new construction–based marketplace, in which eight-foot ceiling heights, modern ranch molding and shag carpeting reigned supreme. Their own collection of recycled house parts, as Connie observed, created a Milwaukee Avenue reuse center. Many of these houses today bear parts from other nearby houses. "And where else could this happen?" she asked.

Harold put his recently acquired carpentry skills to work during the day. He soon discovered that the rear section of the structure had wood framing that was too deteriorated to drive nails into. Harold tore off this part of the house and rebuilt it with new framing. Connie worked her career job. After work, she rode her bicycle to 2204 Milwaukee to join Harold. In their two-person carpentry team, Harold made the measurements and scribed the cut marks on the wood member, and Connie sawed the piece. Harold held one end while Connie nailed it into place. Harold recalled occasional moments of doubt, unsure of whether he was using the right carpentry method for the task at hand. But he was tempered by realizing that "we needed less faith that we could succeed than those first rehabbers."

A few of these early rehabbers, like Harold, were one-year-and-out architecture school students who became innovators in design of their own houses. They integrated modern architectural ideas and newly available products into historic contexts—introducing skylights that could fit appropriately on roof pitches perpendicular to the street. While the façades of these houses retained their original historic character (as did side walls in public view), rear areas could accommodate modern design ideas, such

The rehab of Harold and Connie Fournier's house at 2204 Milwaukee Avenue required tearing down the back part of the structure's decrepit framing.

as a plentitude of windows—for which there was a very practical reason. As Harold and Connie noted, typical Milwaukee Avenue houses were originally built with small rooms, apparently for the purpose of providing some measure of privacy to households of large families. Small windows in sidewalls of these narrow lots inhibited sunlight, and the typically limited illumination of lighting fixtures resulted in relatively dark interiors. Larger rear windows provided opportunities to bring more light into these houses, which were now redesigned with open floor plans.

During their construction process, Harold and Connie found themselves talking to people who once lived in the house when they were young children. Some left notes about memories they had of the house. One morning, Harold came to work and found a shoebox cover with a penciled message reading, "Those were happy days when I lived here—thank you for fixing my house."

Harold and Connie felt that their forebears on Milwaukee Avenue had set up the experience base that drove everyone else's experiences. Somehow the matrix holding everyone together was their unblinking ability to face their unknowns. In Connie's words, "We were too naïve to know how everything would work, but what else could we do in our circumstances? And what we somehow did know was that this was a historical time, and we were part if it."[45]

Blind Faith

In truth, the expertise of many individuals who entered the rehab program could be measured more by their youthful ambition than their carpentry skills. Nonetheless, for IRP people, their ambition fueled doing what it took to learn the skills needed to finish the job. What also helped immensely was the flurry of young would-be carpenters who found themselves within a neighborhood of their peers, eager to facilitate cooperative learning. Even more helpful were building inspectors who, although initially suspicious of these young men, eventually became guiding hands (Sid Swanson, I wish you could be reading this!). HRA staff members found themselves frequently away from their desks and their shoes covered with sawdust, offering rehabbers carpentry advice such as a few tricks on "kerfing" long trim members and laying out the treads and risers of a new stairway (thank you, Chuck Gustafson and Tom Goodoien!).

Some people in the IRP chose to hire contractors to do most of the work. They would sweep up the place every evening and eventually do the painting and other minor projects such as closet shelving. One such couple, Sid and Lola Berg, fell in love with a dilapidated house at 2125 Milwaukee Avenue, whose red brick had been covered over many times with gray paint. Their house was one of the first in the IRP, a time when this experiment in urban renewal was untested and uncertain. They hired Soderberg Construction of St. Paul as their general contractor. The condition of the house varied from troublesome to desperate, but the Bergs were unfazed. While the Soderberg crew stabilized the house's exterior walls, Sid and Lola pulled down all of the brick from the exterior walls, set up planks on sawhorses and used bricklayer hammers to chip mortar off the brick surfaces. Over several weeks' time, Sid and Lola, occasionally joined by neighbors, cleaned more than twelve thousand bricks. Later, Soderberg bricklayers simply refaced the bricks so that the side once facing the framing, now seemingly fresh from decades of being hidden in darkness, faced outward in the sunlit air and in full view.

Many years later, when asked what caused the Bergs to persevere, Lola replied, "Blind faith." And Lola's words rang true for many on Milwaukee Avenue and in Seward West.

In effect, all the rehabilitated houses, as well as those waiting to be rehabilitated, represented a definitive quality standard. Houses that exemplified the attribute of tradition had shifted the value set of this oncoming generation, who disregarded the whole of the twentieth century and its habit of producing the ever new. In this previous milieu, tradition was defined as what had become obsolete.

CHAPTER 17

Legal Snafus:
Forming the Homeowners Association

In the final months of 1976, several MACC and IRP houses were nearing completion, and many others were imminent. Meanwhile, legal groundwork establishing the homeowners association was occurring. At first, HRA and PAC saw this as unproblematic and necessary, as the various association rules and stipulations in their basic form were well understood. But early into the legal process, a big and nasty snafu happened.

Before a homeowners association could be chartered, HRA, which had taken ownership of all of the residential properties in the four-block area, began the process of verifying clear property titles. A crucial aspect of this work was verifying property lines, which opened up a hornet's nest. Original block surveys describing overall north–south measurements were slightly skewed to be more narrow by a few inches at the south end, while individual property plat lines carried identical dimensions instead of minutely more narrow dimensions following the lineup of lots from south to north. These inaccuracies were miniscule but legally troublesome.

HRA commissioned the re-platting surveys to correct these 1880s deviations, which was technically feasible but involved due diligence of the history of previous property surveys and owners. This is where the legal horror show began. The re-platting uncovered the realization that innumerable tiny slivers of property were unknowingly transferred to many property owners from 1880s origins to the present day. As a result, uncountable numbers of dead people held fractions of legal titles to many of these properties. The proper legal protocol was to halt development of properties without a clear title. These legal problems put the formation of the homeowners association on hold.

When HRA legal staff uncovered this situation, they knew development was underway and that it would affect many properties with suspect titles. HRA attorney Mike Schwab, with whom who I had enjoyed a jovial working relationship, called me and laid out the situation. "The HRA and PAC can proceed with rehabilitating the houses now underway," Mike told me, " but at the authority's peril." He described how the appropriate move would be to suspend development while the legal work ran its course. "Why did you present me with this predicament?" I asked Mike. "My job is simply to draw lines." I asked him this tongue in cheek knowing that Mike, as well as others in HRA, acknowledged my role complementing Tony Scallon as the prime movers of the whole Milwaukee Area scenario. So I told him I'd talk to the big guy.

I then visited Tony and outlined the situation as Mike Schwab had constructed it. Tony asked me what I would do if it were my decision. I quickly thought to myself that with a development project the nature of this one, with all its sometimes-bewildering complexity, any delay in physical advancement might invite factors that could change and diminish what has been envisioned. A restart could be problematic. "Let's keep development underway. Then let the lawyers have their turn," I answered. "That's what lawyers are for—to make the legal underpinnings hold everything together." Tony agreed and called Mike. Tony's directive to Mike was enough to keep the agency from suspending progress.

That decision soon proved to greatly exacerbate HRA's administrative process, which PAC already had made much more difficult with its multifaceted and complicated four-block-area development plan. The problem of the entangled property lines took an extreme amount of time to solve, as HRA and its consulting legal firm had to backtrack previous property owners and their property transfers over a seventy-year period. This meant that HRA could not sell properties on which houses had recently been renovated by MACC or to individual rehabbers who had been working on their houses for a long time. So HRA arranged to rent these houses to the buyers and rehab parties until the legal process could guarantee clear titles, which varied property by property for several months to over a year. But to halt momentum of the rehab process would have likely stultified the niche market that had been so successful.

House by house, rehab continued, both in the IRP and MACC. But as HRA held titles to these houses, when the work was completed, they did not have clear titles until past ownerships could be resolved. Due diligence was the term describing legal searches attempting to track down heirs of former owners by making a determined search, but successfully locating all possible owners of these tiny land fragments was impossible. So public agency attorneys defined a particular search method, posted public notices and took other steps in trying to solve the problem. One method used by HRA was publishing a legal notice in a local publication asking all former property owners to respond (but of course the deceased former property owners were unable to do so).

One by one, properties were given clear titles and then transferred to the new rehabber-owners when they completed their redevelopment contract with HRA. This process resulted in significant complications to HRA's administration of the renewal program, and occasionally PAC heard grumbling of how this process had "put the cart before the horse." But we were undaunted. And as the renewal program proceeded, HRA found itself in occasional financial shortfalls. Funding for the Milwaukee Avenue walkway, with its ornamental lighting, landscaping and other enhancements, had been committed before these imbalances were realized. Therefore, a delay for the sake of legal order might have short-circuited these amenities that gave the area its extraordinary ambience.

But legal problems affecting land were not over. Another significant obstacle occurred after the homeowners association legal work resumed. The law firm that HRA contracted to write the Milwaukee Avenue Area Homeowners Association deed covenants seemed, in its first attempt, to rely mostly on boilerplate technical provisions that were not workable in several major sections. Homeowner associations recently enacted at that time were town house developments in which the homeowners held ownership of the land under their units while the surrounding land was held in common, or "undivided interest," by association members, with covenants attached to each owner's deed. These covenants also obligated each owner to association membership and related by-laws that set forth parking considerations, use of dedicated space adjacent to each dwelling unit, adherence to architectural controls for the unit exteriors and other provisions that enforced a necessary architectural conformity.

A second attempt was also infeasible. PAC staff, meaning Jeri and I, spent much time in meetings and phone calls with the attorney in charge, and our points relating to particular aspects of the four-block area were at first deemed unworkable. We pointed out that this was no typical homeowners association. Major differences were needed for individual ownership of the houses to include the properties within the related boundary lines. While the houses on Milwaukee Avenue were part of a historic district, the houses on Twenty-second and Twenty-third Avenues were not and required slightly different architectural controls. In addition, the pedestrian walkway required a public-use permit even though it was owned by the association. Many of these factors were unique to this situation, and the HRA attorneys did not want a typical boilerplate to specify what it was not able to do. The lengthy delays hampered progress until the law firm finally devised the correct legal documents.

CHAPTER 18
Designing the New to Fit with the Old

The quickly realized popularity of rehabilitation that occurred on Milwaukee Avenue and in the rest of the Seward West neighborhood demonstrably influenced the architectural design of new houses built following the first wave of rehab. Nine new houses built on vacant lots on Milwaukee Avenue were exact replicas of rehabilitated houses. And in the heart of the neighborhood beyond, contemporary architectural design for new houses failed to take hold. Instead, these new houses continued the neighborhood's traditional architecture in the form of steep roofs with gables facing the street, narrow lap siding, wide trim, open front porches and vertically oriented double-hung windows.

As noted, Milwaukee Avenue sat in the midst of an architectural transition, just after the modern movement put its dogmatic high-style capital into architecture committed to the social capital of urban change. In 1976, as rehab on Milwaukee Avenue was in full swing, AEI Architects designed and built a pair of side-by-side town houses on two cleared lots on the middle of Milwaukee Avenue, followed by three additional pairs facing East Twenty-second Street and Twenty-second Avenue. AEI's design represents that transition; the architectural expression of the structures is unmistakably mid-1970s, with its modern design approach paying respect to the historical district.

As rehab progressed, its success became noticeably apparent. This buzz of five or six houses always under rehab contrasted the slumping housing industry, hampered by a national economy in recession and bedeviled by

New side-by-side town houses fill in the spot formerly occupied by houses that were unfit for rehab and subsequently razed.

extraordinarily high interest rates. By the summer of 1976, demand had increased for vacant Milwaukee Avenue houses.

JUST SAY YES TO ORNAMENT

Modernism represented a period in history when the use of ornament was briefly suspended.
—*Arthur Drexler, former director of the Department of Architecture at the Museum of Modern Art, New York*

The University of Minnesota's School of Architecture placed high emphasis on modernism, from institutional and commercial building types to residential design. A sizable portion of the architectural practice in the general market hewed to the tried and true. But for everyone in architecture school in the 1960s and '70s, modernism was the religion of architecture, and its true believers accepted nothing else.

Outside the four-block area, the first group of cleared lots in Seward West was located in a two-block section extending from the southeast corner of the renewal area. These lots became home sites for longtime Seward West residents who chose new, package-type new houses intended for the suburbs. These residents, fortified with the HRA purchase of their house and a $20,000 grant toward purchasing their next house, built the first new houses in Seward West on these recently cleared lots. The fact that these relocatees wanted to stay in the neighborhood and build new homes was considered by HRA as one of the successes of the renewal program. The people had lived in old houses all their lives and now, in their remaining years, wanted new houses like those of their offspring in the suburbs. With that mindset, they chose new one-story ramblers and split-levels constructed by package-house builders. This was not what PAC wanted to see, but it was important to respect the decisions of the long-term neighborhood residents.

After a dozen or so of these ranchers were built in this area of the neighborhood, new houses with traditional architectural design were built on newly cleared lots. There were two factors in this change. Typically, younger people had become attracted to the neighborhood because it gave them an opportunity to rehab an older house. When these older houses started gaining new life, it quickly set a traditional standard for new residential dwellings that could complement this historic neighborhood.

New Life: Rehabbers Set Up Housekeeping

After the paint was dry, the dishes were in the cupboards and the same second-hand furniture they had lived with before renewal was set in place, these homeowners made themselves at home. Now they could read their past issues of the *Whole Earth Catalog* with some sense of leisure. Having accomplished something major in their lives, it now seemed time to rest. Their houses were finished, but getting their yards in shape could wait a while. The grass had long been worn away by construction activity, and shrubs and flowerbeds had been knocked down and crushed.

The yards of MACC houses were finished with four inches of black dirt raked over the sandy soil, followed by the placement of sod and a long period of watering. For the individual rehabbers, a psychological time-out seemed necessary. But a year or two later came the summer of landscaping, and the neighborhood gained that final touch of renewal.

In later phases of the overall rehab process, Greater Minneapolis Metropolitan Housing Corporation, an area-wide nonprofit organization,

2012 Milwaukee Avenue is one of ten wood-clad single-family houses on the avenue. The exterior's Victorian Stick influences were thoroughly preserved during the early 1970s renovation, while its interior was refashioned into a more contemporary design.

sponsored rehabilitation of four units; HRA rehabilitated two houses; and Seward West Redesign rehabilitated five duplexes on Twenty-second Avenue.

The IRP was considered one of its successes as the means for homeowners to reduce the cost of providing a house for themselves, tailored to their needs and desires. In time, however, came the realization that this process accounted for more houses saved than what otherwise might have happened. Contrary to previous public agency expectations, over time, the older character of rehabilitated houses attracted higher real estate sales than did new houses. And in a larger context, IRP proved to be the most effective form of affordable housing, ennobled by the accomplishment of creating one's own shelter. And thus a neighborhood was appropriately re-created by many people who did the work of rebuilding with their own hands.

BECOMING A NEIGHBORHOOD AGAIN

Houses rehabilitated by MACC on Milwaukee Avenue and Twenty-second Avenue quickly found new buyers, many of whom moved in from other parts of the Twin Cities area and fit right in with the rehabbers. Similar to the original PAC members, these buyers possessed a new values consciousness, with no dependence on continual consumption as a basis for

A row of rehabilitated Milwaukee Avenue duplexes completed during the years 1978–81.

The structure at 2311 Twenty-second Avenue is one of several duplexes in the Milwaukee Avenue Four-Block Area that underwent thorough exterior and interior rehabilitation in the late 1970s.

personal fulfillment. Specifically, these smaller houses fit their aspirations. The incoming people created varied households, and those with children were rare. Gradually, a few couples started families. The walkway gained the cheerful noise of kids on their tricycles, pulling little wagons, and the mini park became busy with parents and their kids. Springtime brought flowers, as

A side-by-side townhouse on Twenty-second Avenue built in the late 1970s complements nearby late nineteenth-century duplexes. An architecturally important aspect of the new structure is its ability to fit the existing streetscape without giving the building a false sense of history.

fewer and fewer yards had to double as construction sites. Halloween trick-or-treaters resumed their haunts along Milwaukee Avenue, and the mail carrier again had mailboxes to fill. Eventually, approximately twenty-one of the thirty-six rehabilitated houses on Milwaukee Avenue were completed under the IRP, as well as another twenty-six properties on Twenty-second and Twenty-third Avenues. Elsewhere in Seward West, individual rehabbers accounted for well over one hundred houses.

The political machinery of PAC still needed to hum for a while, as there were still administrative actions left to perform. But as PAC began to realize that its work was nearing completion, it made the moves it needed to, and sometime in the mid-1980s, the last person turned out the lights and locked the door. Many other Minneapolis urban renewal neighborhood project area committees found ways to perpetuate themselves, but the Seward West PAC could not see itself turn into a bureaucracy.

CHAPTER 19

Milwaukee Avenue Today

LIVING ON THE AVENUE

Diane Richard
July 9, 2011

After dinner one autumn evening a few years back, my husband and I snapped on the dog's leash and set out for a stroll. The sun was falling in the sky, and the streetlights were flickering on. We rounded the corner onto Milwaukee Avenue. From our vantage point near the public garden, we saw two strangers sitting on our porch bench. Were they lost? Drunk? Members of the Kingdom Hall down the block? We sidled up. "Can we help you?" I asked from my front steps. "Uh, you live here?" replied one of the fellows, a stout man about sixty years of age. I nodded. Shrugging toward his friend, he said, "We thought this was a tourist attraction."

We've lived on Milwaukee Avenue since 1998, attracted by its central location, pedestrian street and brick workman's cottages dating to the 1880s. Most newcomers to the block marvel at this urban sanctuary and, notably, our ability to live without, for many of the homes, garages. I marvel at how anyone could abide a car parked in front of their house or—the horror!—driving down the street.

Our greened-in street was one of many strokes of genius integral to the late-1970s rehabilitation of Milwaukee Avenue. Others are the houses themselves, a tantalizing combination of new and old. Many architectural elements are original, like our brick exterior and wicked-steep main staircase, though the mechanicals, walls, windows and foundation take advantage of twentieth-century technology. So do the popcorn ceilings. And the bad '70s track lighting. And the *Boogie Nights* bathroom on our second floor. In many ways, that bathroom—arguably larger than almost any in the city limits—was the hinge to a healthy marriage and functional household. Let me explain. The previous homeowner blew out the second bedroom on the top floor to expand the tiny bathroom and install a four-person cedar-sided hot tub, not unlike the ones you'd find outdoors in California (clink the wine coolers). That remodeling aberration necessitated the bedrooms of my stepsons to be installed in the finished basement, thereby sanctifying a domestic separation of church and state, with the first floor serving as a common space. I tried never to go to the basement; they came upstairs to use the shower and, years later, take really, really long baths in the six-foot-long cast-iron tub (after we Sawzall-ed out the hot tub).

This unique block, built to quadruple density by a greedy developer a century before the phrase "new urbanism" was ever uttered, exercises its considerable charms with modest understatement. On any other street, few but perhaps the most immediate of neighbors know one another by name. I know the names of nearly every neighbor in every house down all four blocks, those of their kids and pets and, in many cases, those of the parents who visit from far away, as well as the babysitters and nannies. Blocks with front-porch sitters, dog walkers, coffee drinkers and active association members make for a close-knit neighborhood.

I sometimes liken this place to a kibbutz. Upon our arrival, our neighbors greeted us with a cake and welcome party, and lively backyard barbecues ensued. Compost turners, free-range eggs, Japanese language lessons and subscriptions to the *Economist* are all ripe to be shared. But this is no bucolic utopia. There are shy people, nice-enough non-participators and damaged people and jerks, just like everywhere else. For instance, we lived here for a decade before ever glimpsing the men who occupy the immaculate home across the street—a distance so close I could hit it with water from my hose if I held my finger over the nozzle. Three years later, I saw them again (or at least I thought it was them) sitting on their porch. I had no idea what to say. What do you say to people who opt not to wade in the glue—block parties, semiannual cleanups, community governance or idle chitchat—that holds neighborhoods together? I smiled and, like Dionne Warwick, walked on by.

You know the saying about how tall fences make good neighbors? Well, our fences are mandated to be no taller than forty-two inches. Historic?

COMMUNITY RENEWAL IN MINNEAPOLIS

Yes. Awkward? On occasion. Still, I've come to realize that—guess what?—introverted and difficult people existed a century ago, too, so they, too, are doing their part to maintain the block's historical integrity. I myself often retreat to the side patio, shrouded from the front sidewalk by a forsythia tree, a slender stand of birch and robust wild sumac. My husband, Todd, prefers to sprawl on our front porch bench, eager for conversation and "What's the story of this block?" inquiries. Then, after signing the mortgage papers, many work to subvert it.

My first act was to install a hand-towel dispenser, which I purchased at a downtown department store's closing sale, as a mailbox. It had a mirror so that you could check your lipstick while you wipe your hands, though I doubt any postal carrier ever took advantage of it. A few years of constant exposure later, it had rusted to a junkyard patina, and I replaced it with a copper mailbox that's much less of an eyesore. My neighbors were too good-natured to say anything, at least while I was in earshot. Other residents fancy themselves in Tuscany, creating little alfresco patios with fancy iron frou-frous. A sculptor who worked in bowling balls left his mark. Some suburban-sized garages have sprung up like massive boils. And fire pits and cherimoyas run amok.

To the neighborhood association's architectural review committee (ARC), on which I serve, such embellishments are known as "personal expression," which we attempt to curb with pleas to maintain harmony. Though most comply in good nature, some homeowners scoff at having to seek approval for exterior modifications; presumably, the historical authenticity that attracted them eventually becomes a buzz kill. Yet when one lives in a historic district, it's important to remember history is living, not embalmed. The original inhabitants would scratch their heads at our stubborn refusal to evolve, though that is what we've agreed to, within certain preservationist parameters. On flanking avenues, a few absentee landlords are proving the cynical stereotype, allowing renters to trash their homes and yards with cigarette butts, busted bicycles, rotting wood and faded blankets covering the windows. Out of sight and mind, they practice a special brand of malicious neglect that makes city living such a mixed bag. Despite them, most residents—homeowners and renters both—are fiercely devoted to life on this four-block stretch.

National Night Out is a massive outpouring of chips and salsa, quinoa and organic hot dogs, watermelon and rhubarb crisp. Spontaneous games of croquet break out on the Twenty-second Street green space, drawing all comers. Bicycle bells ring merrily as riders exalt in safe passage. In winter, freshly fallen snow is soon laced with cross-country ski trails, both adult and child sized. Generations of children have called the Tot Lot's train station their own. And chalk art makes the public sidewalks a washable Sistine Chapel.

Neighborhood amenities have only improved in the past few years. Light-rail transit is a quick hike down Franklin Avenue, offering access to the new Twins stadium, the Lake Street YWCA and, with a stop at the airport, the whole wide world. The other way down Franklin is the Seward Co-op, recently expanded to include a fabulous meat market. And ten minutes on a bike will get you more fresh farmer's market produce than you could eat in a week. Former residents are among the legions of "walk and gawkers" who flock to the block. It's fun to hear their stories, though I could've done without hearing how someone's aunt died in what is now my bedroom. They marvel at how "cute" the block has become after the profound "shabbifying" the houses took on in the '60s and '70s. A *Star Tribune* article in 1972 proclaimed Milwaukee Avenue as having "some of the sorriest-looking, most decrepit decaying houses in Minneapolis." The period pictures show little but blight. So, too, the flames of fierce resolve. The author of this book, Bob Roscoe, was one of the preservation champions able to see beauty through the cracked stucco, concealed front porches and gaping orifices. That the Seward West PAC fought for a decade to salvage the block from the city's "renewal" plans—and won—is a triumph. Today, these historic and infill homes tell a new story. Where they once sheltered hippies and students and working-class folks, they now harbor professors, lawyers, technology entrepreneurs, artists, videographers, nurses and one high-ranking cop. Pedestrian-friendly historic preservation comes at a premium these days.

We raised a family here, as so many others did before us. Though the houses are small by some standards, we found that 1,900 square feet (including the finished basement) was ample. I've heard as many as eleven immigrant men initially occupied these homes. Where they slept and ate and moved their bowels is a wonder. What they would think of our dishwashers, Wi-Fi and central HVAC is equally mysterious. Of the East African residents who populate Franklin Avenue, strolling in tie-dye burqas and drinking coffee in local coffee shops, unimaginable. Now that our boys have moved out, Todd and I ramble around in what feels like a luxury of space. We've never missed having a garage, which I contend is merely a repository of broken dehumidifiers and "someday" sports equipment. Our dog rules the universe—or at least our tiny kingdom. There's no telling what the future holds, but I can see us here for many more years.

CHAPTER 20
Finding What It Means

The automobile has not merely taken over the street; it has dissolved the living tissue of the city.
—James Marston Fitch, architectural historian

In 1977, architect and theorist Christopher Alexander wrote his epochal book *A Pattern Language*, in which he stated that the various parts of the built landscape—towns, streets, buildings, etc.—should be considered as elements within ordered relationships rather than separate structures. When we planned the Milwaukee Avenue Four-Block Area a few years before, Alexander's later-to-be-published principles, such as hierarchy of public to private space, were already in place. The sequence of spaces from the public walkway to front porches and the dwellings themselves provide maximum usability. The minimal setbacks of the house's façades serve to "shape the outdoors." In Alexander's words, "On no account allow setbacks between streets or paths or public open land and the buildings which front on them."

According to Alexander, in the public residential streetscape, house façades should be considered not simply as fronts of structures whose walls are cut out for windows and doors but as having a relationship with the structured shelter, front yard and street. He observes that the level of vehicular traffic on a street affects how people feel about their home territory. Heavy traffic creates a less personal connection, affecting how they feel about the other houses along the street. Lightly traveled streets allow for an appreciation of street life and help create a sense of community.

These associations extend in complexity and in their relationship to streetscapes in various modes: solids to space, shelter to land, outside to inside. But the role of architecture exists as something more complicated and nuanced than that, as forms of a house in relation to landscape can invite perceptions of personal relationships. These relationships invite us with the sense of the familiarity, those archetypal forms based on tradition. Porches evoke a sense of appeal, simple and open shelter structure made graceful by their ornamental display. Many Milwaukee Avenue porches were built exactly the same, but today, all sorts of individual and personal appurtenances now define who lives inside. Porches are an example of transitions in architecture that form the relationships described by Alexander. In a seeming contradiction, they are both cozy and completely open to public space just beyond. Porches welcome us as we prepare to enter the dwelling or greet passersby.

NEW URBANISM

New urbanism has become a planning option for wise land use in cities and for new development in suburban areas, becoming somewhat of a conservation practice in itself. New urbanism reintroduces traditional living patterns of time-honored principles that have existed for many centuries. It brings people and resources into a codependent relationship, which is ultimately the best form of sustainability. Architects have quickly found favor with new urbanism, as it fosters the design of human scale in the built environment.

The layout of the Milwaukee Avenue Four-Block Area existed nearly a century before the advent of new urbanism. In comparing Milwaukee Avenue to new urbanism, both feature walkable environments that set limits on autos, dedicated public open space and residential units in compact clusters, often as an anomaly within the conventional city grid. An important distinction, however, is that the architecture of new urbanism depends on the configuration of geometric forms for its aesthetic value. Milwaukee Avenue houses, smaller in comparison, offer fine details in the form of spindle friezes, lathe-turned columns and gable filigree panels. New urbanism sites are multi-directional, while Milwaukee Avenue is linear. The houses on Milwaukee Avenue feature simplicity as well as complexity, which vernacular architecture offers in counterpart with articulated detail,

The articulated geometry of Milwaukee Avenue ornament makes sun and shadow heighten their architectural presence. The succession of the other workman's cottages along the street gives Milwaukee Avenue a charming character that is unique among other vernacular neighborhoods in Minneapolis and St. Paul, as well as the rest of the country.

giving a more intimate sense of relationship to people who live and walk down the street.

As to new urbanism's emphasis on reducing auto dependence, several examples can be mentioned here, one of which is the conversion of Milwaukee Avenue to a vehicle-free pedestrian walkway. Its direct connection with Franklin Avenue at the street's northern end gives access to several bus lines, as well as the Hiawatha Avenue Light Rail. The Midtown Greenway bike route is two blocks away. This stretch of Franklin Avenue contains five popular cafés, an exercise studio, two coffee houses, several ethnic grocery stores, a liquor store and a co-op grocery store. Many local artists have studios within walking distance and participate in annual neighborhood art fairs.

Architect Chuck Levin and his wife, Lynn, a jewelry artist, have lived on Milwaukee Avenue for over twenty years. Both work in their respective lower-level and first-floor studios, with their living accommodations on the second floor and loft area above. A very small but significant feature of their house, the couple remarks, is the worn staircase, which features marks from the boots of workers who lived in the home during its early years.

Living and working on Milwaukee Avenue has offered Levin many discoveries about urban spaces and the houses within, all giving preservation a value for living. "Nobody builds houses this small anymore," he observes, "But people live on this street because they are buying a neighborhood as much as a house, and community values are what makes this area such a great place to live. The landscape makes such a large difference. Walking down the street, you see the wonderful variety of the homeowners' individual gardening plots, which doesn't happen in planned residential communities. Much of new urbanism is multi-unit development, where uniform landscaping is mandated." Looking out his studio window or from his front porch, Levin occasionally sees people walking down Milwaukee Avenue apparently for the first time. "They walk along, stop and then turn their heads to face what they are looking at. They repeat this several times," he said, noting how the visitors become captured by the uniqueness of the area.

Levin places a particular importance on what preservation offers that is often absent in new urbanism. The authenticity of materials becomes the indelible attribute of older buildings' significance. "Here, we don't see Trex porch decking, aluminum siding, metal storm doors and that certain 'plastic quality.'" He notes another less obvious aspect of preservation and his bearing on Milwaukee Avenue, which isn't found in the architecture of new urbanism. "Here, it is a hundred little things that were done right," Levin commented. "Nowhere else can you see this."

Lessons Lost, Lessons Learned

Dick Brustad, who became director of the Minneapolis HRA during the time when PAC took control of Seward West, had the following to say about Milwaukee Avenue's effect on the city: "Seward West was so important in many ways, especially the preservation of Milwaukee Avenue. But from the perspective of the City of Minneapolis, it was also an important milestone because it changed its way of thinking about urban renewal. The community taught the city that deteriorated neighborhoods could be successfully rehabilitated rather than always razed through the process of urban renewal." The question often asked today, invariably during tours of Milwaukee Avenue, is, "Could this be repeated today?" There are many factors in place today that did not exist in the 1970s.[46]

Lessons Lost

PAC members' sense of purpose was so strong that much personal sacrifice was expended to achieve the organization's goal, although this occurred during a time when many of today's societal distractions did not exist. Its individual members, along with many Seward West residents of that time, formed a fealty to the overall causes of the day. Moreover, certain governmental factors that allowed the success of Seward West and Milwaukee Avenue no longer exist. Seward West was the last of the area-wide urban renewal programs in the nation, and just when this program figured out how citizens could determine their own destiny, the government ended it. The government's urban renewal toolbox was replaced by what local authorities describe as specially directed surgical applications to micro-areas. The result has been a scattered implementation of renewal, which has drastically vitiated its impact.

Moreover, the federal funding that seemed to be a constantly running, wide-open faucet in the 1970s began to slow the stream of money when Milwaukee Avenue was nearing completion. Eminent domain, a major tool that provided for the acquisition of blighted property, became more selectively applied. These factors, coupled with the zeitgeist-provoked idealism of today's populace, make another Milwaukee Avenue very unlikely. To reinforce this point, no similar development has since occurred in this area or, to our knowledge, anywhere else.

On a comparative basis, city and federal government spend far less money on urban renewal today than what was expended in the early 1970s. This situation exists despite the massive corrosive effects on some city neighborhoods in the era of bank-foreclosed properties. Demolition once again is the tool of choice for public agencies overseeing stability of urban neighborhoods. The "new affordability" of Seward West in the 1970s could have its equivalent today in several urban American neighborhoods. That affordability is strained by city agencies coming to grips with rising inventories of dilapidated and abandoned housing. In the 1970s, concentrating agency resources in a coordinated resolve, with the IRP and city-assisted reduced-interest homeowner loans, proved effective, embraced by city building inspectors who became problem solvers instead of inflexible regulation enforcers. Today, the will to revive these practices seems absent.

Adding to this situation is the fact that the successes of neighborhood nonprofit organizations that revitalized neighborhoods with relatively cost-effective rehabilitation are no longer potent today. These homegrown housing incubators have been replaced by what have become generic metropolitan-based nonprofits that have easy access to city agency personnel and their funding sources and are supported by various corporate interests that presume their funding is doing social good. Certainly, many of the former neighborhood nonprofits were a bit hyperactive at times, but more creative housing solutions came out of them than have from their tranquilized replacements.

Some public agencies have reversed several decades of activist citizens who gained genuine decision-making roles in collaborative processes with their public agency overseers and now have little appetite to listen to the residents they serve. Their bureaucrats have developed a complex regulatory framework and have also learned to be more sustainable than neighborhood leaders. Among the challenges faced by today's housing market are increased building code regulations and construction costs. Bank financing is difficult, as it was in the 1970s, but city programs to supply homeownership are scant and strapped with an overabundance of requirements.

A very critical component of house rehabilitation in Seward West was the IRP, which made a critical difference in opening up the number of repairable houses to qualified would-be homeowners. Today, the opportunity for substantial individual rehab is not permitted by many city public agencies.

Lessons Learned

Milwaukee Avenue began a movement to honor the history of people whose muscle and sweat built our nation and to preserve their vernacular houses. The age of citizen activism has since expanded to provide important change to urban environments. The craft of rehabilitation in historic context, largely developed in Seward West, has contributed to how older and historic houses are saved, albeit on a much higher per-house construction cost. Neighborhood organizations today typically regard the reuse of older buildings as a default policy, replacing the former sentiment of "new is the only answer."

From a cultural standpoint, the early 1970s was a phenomenal period of change in American history, with one of the attributes of its standard-bearers being their lack of concern for what was in it for them. For them, it was about the betterment of overall society, which they saw as their individual benefits.

The post–World War II shift to leaving urban areas for the suburbs is now reversing itself. In the economic times and real estate market of the beginning of the second decade of the twenty-first century, Christopher Leinberger, professor of urban and regional planning, sees the overbuilt and unsold housing inventories of certain suburban and ex-urban areas, along with the recent stability in walkable urban areas, as signs that "we are shifting our slums to the fringe of our metropolitan areas." Leinberger states that the trend is already in place for "walkable environments that are far more energy efficient and environmentally sustainable."[47]

CHAPTER 21

The Need for Rediscovering Walkable Communities

With a centrally located green space or commons, in lieu of a street down the middle, and with a clearly and elegantly demarcated entrance into the neighborhood, a collective identity is created. Before long, neighbors get to know each other and provide for each other the kind of community support system that family members across town, across state or across country cannot. It is the opportunity for informal interactions allowing people to get to know their neighbors, and it is these interactions that provide the roots for true community to flourish.
—*Sarah Susanka, as quoted in Ross Chapin's* Pocket Neighborhoods

Bruce Margolis and his wife, Carol, do not live on Milwaukee Avenue. But they do live on nearby Twenty-second Avenue and belong to the Milwaukee Avenue Four-Block Area's homeowners association. For both of them, closely grouped houses mean closely grouped neighbors.

If we were asked how many of our neighbors would instinctively agree to drive us to the airport, most of us could come up with maybe a handful. These would be people living no more than a few doors away. But for Bruce, this question becomes, "How big is the boundary of area residents I could ask?" But Bruce comments, "Well, there are a few new people who recently moved in who I don't know well enough yet."

Throughout the centuries, talking with your neighbors was a highly uncomplicated and unconscious act—you saw your neighbor walking past your house and, depending on which impulse you instantly dialed into your mind, you waved and said, "Hi, how are you?" Or if you had a bit of news on the tip of your tongue, you might have been eager to talk for a few minutes. Or perhaps it was a time to simply smile and nod and go on with what you were doing. On Milwaukee Avenue, this ritual happens effortlessly all the time. The proximity of porches a few feet away from the walkway brings many neighbors in closer connection with one another.

A new form of development in neighborhood formation is appearing at the edges of many cities and towns, where common spaces allow people to rediscover a sense of community. In *Pocket Neighborhoods*, an interesting book written by architect-author Ross Chapin, he describes these small-scale communities:

> *Shared outdoor space is a key element of a pocket neighborhood. It is neither private (home/yard) nor public (a busy street, park) but rather a defined space between the private and public realms. The residents surrounding this common space share its care and oversight, thereby enhancing a felt and actual sense of security and identity. Because of its location and design, the shared outdoor space fosters interaction among neighbors, which, in time, may grow into deeper, long-term relationships.*[48]

Chapin included Milwaukee Avenue in his book, stating that the success of the campaign to save it and develop its character is described in a Chinese proverb: "Perseverance furthers with a generous amount of community spirit." Perhaps serendipity could be added to this proverb, as the confluence of certain forces that came about in the 1970s was critical.

Milwaukee Avenue fits perfectly into the definition of a pocket neighborhood. The best urban spaces encourage diverse urban experiences and community coordination based on shared interests. Milwaukee Avenue is a public realm; it is not owned by the government but rather the community around it. Milwaukee Avenue can be accessed from four different areas, with no gates to restrict anyone. In this way, it shares status with some of the nation's more recognized open walkable spaces, such as the Capitol Mall in Washington, D.C., and the Rockefeller Center and High Line in New York City.

Transportation technologies have set patterns for cities since ancient times. Urban economist Edward Glaeser observed that cities like Jerusalem and Florence became walking cities; midtown Manhattan and the Chicago loop were built around trains and elevators.[49] Twentieth-century cities such as Los Angeles determined urban form on the ways in which cars could most efficiently travel and where they could be parked. Ubiquitous auto use limits the ways in which people can best enjoy their environments and lessens the quality of the air we breathe. Until now, these impairments in our everyday life have been taken for granted.

Accumulating evidence that automobile exhaust is a well-known significant cause of air pollution, along with escalating gasoline costs, traffic congestion and the limits to continuing suburban expansion, is evident. So, too, is the obvious fact that city dwellers drive less. Less obvious is the acknowledgement that in reducing carbon emissions, high-efficiency cars are not nearly as important as miles less traveled. All of these factors are beginning to have effects on real estate, as the mantra of high property values based on "location, location, location" is being replaced by "location, efficiency, livability."

The Great Inversion, a book by Alan Ehrenhalt, executive director of Stateline, a daily news site operated by the Pew Research Center, offers a similar statement: "We are living at a moment in which the massive outward migration of the affluent that characterized the second half of the twentieth century is coming to an end." He also notes that cities are no longer experiencing immigrants starting their lives in the central city, which has been the classic pattern in America throughout most of its history. These groups are instead finding their homes in the suburbs.

What is causing the shift? Ehrenhalt notes that cities have become more appealing for the affluent, a principal reason being deindustrialization. Most of the nation's cities began as industrial centers for heavy manufacturing, built for factories and their workers, with resultant smokestacks and railroad trackage near many residential neighborhoods. The post–world war suburban surge dramatically transformed residential patterns. Recently, cities have significantly removed large industries and the clutter of ancillary facilities, allowing city planning departments to rezone these sites to create more pleasant environments and higher-density housing. With the growth of theaters, museums, parks, cleaner air and seemingly endless choices of large and small restaurants, cities have become attractive places to live.

Moving through our cities is also undergoing transformation. While the car may remain a main form of transportation, it is now one of many choices and no longer the typical means. Light-rail transit, bicycles and the reemergence of streetcars are becoming popular, causing city planning departments to give incentives for developers who locate housing along or nearby main transit routes to reduce the size of parking areas. Cities are now competing to become the most walkable and the most bikeable in the nation. These once-alternative transit modes are changing urban patterns that portend more integrated residential use with walkable environments.

According to Richard Florida's April 20, 2012 *Atlantic* magazine article, "Cities Place Matters," in 2009, people between the ages of sixteen and thirty-four took 24 percent more bike trips than they took in 2001 and walked to their destinations 16 percent more often, while passenger miles on transit jumped by 40 percent. Part of the reason for this shift is financial, Florida notes, with car ownership a significant burden at the income level of many people in this age group. These people have increased their use of public transit by 100 percent, biking by 122 percent and walking by 37 percent.

The shift away from the car is part of a new way of life being embraced by young Americans, which places less emphasis on big cars or big houses as status symbols or life essentials. Florida wrote, "More and more people are ditching their cars and taking public transit or moving to more walkable neighborhoods, where they can get by without them or by occasionally using a rental car or Zipcar."

A study by J.D. Power and Associates, well known for its automobile rankings, quotes veteran auto industry analyst John Casesa. "There's a cultural change taking place," said Casesa. "It's partly because of the severe economic contraction. But younger consumers are viewing an automobile with a jaundiced eye. They don't view the car the way their parents did, and they don't have the money that their parents did."

In an opinion piece for the *New York Times*, Christopher B. Leinberger summarized a report he coauthored for the Brookings Institution. The report demonstrates the correlation between walkability and real estate value, noting that "real estate values increase as neighborhoods became more walkable, where everyday needs, including working, can be met by walking, transit or biking. These real estate values show increases of more than $300 per month to apartment rents and nearly $82 per square foot to home values."

The Milwaukee Avenue Four-Block Area, from its 1880s origins through its 1970s redevelopment and up to the present day, seems like an anomaly when compared to typical urban neighborhoods. Since the 1970s, countless thousands of people have walked along its commons, appreciating its presence as an irregularity, and many would say this is what makes the place so special.

But this "special" quality should be replicated not detail by detail but with patterns. It should create a small-scaled definable place with appropriately small houses facing (as Christopher Alexander would like) a commons area with walking surfaces landscaping and convenient peripheral parking.

At the University of Minnesota School of Architecture, architect and instructor Dale Mulfinger's studio design class used pocket neighborhoods as a guide for a student design project. After visiting Milwaukee Avenue, each of the four teams was given very small urban sites with tight boundary constraints (less than an acre in size and capable of a maximum of sixteen to eighteen units) located near public transit and bike paths. The students used industrially fabricated housing units capable of being interpreted with individual design features, as well as on-site add-on elements that could be transported to the site. Each module, typically twenty feet wide by thirty-two feet in length and capable of being combined or stacked, is sited around a commons area with nearby parking. Mulfinger described its prospective inhabitants as "those who seek a smaller footprint on the earth."

Pocket neighborhoods can be collectives of small footprints on the earth. They can be places where we can feel our full measure instead of functioning subservient to a large-scale urban living environment. While various healthy living programs are currently promoting healthy foods, walking paths and bicycle routes, these exist somewhat separately from the places in which we spend our most critical time—our homes and neighborhoods. This is where pocket neighborhoods become important. The active promotion of health-related activities as part of urban patterns represents a fundamental shift in how future cities function. In this way, American cities might be undergoing their next transformation. Cities were formed as walking-based centers in agrarian societies of pre-industrial days and became manufacturing citadels in the nineteenth century. American cities may continue their functions as social service networks, increasing cultural infrastructure, while rediscovering and reconstructing themselves, creating a higher degree of well-being for their citizens.

The Milwaukee Avenue Four-Block-Area model has proved to be very successful on the basis of real estate values, urban livability and local history.

In the 1880s, when William Ragan chose to re-plat two typical Minneapolis city blocks to lay out an unorthodox housing plan to maximize his investment, Milwaukee Avenue began its life as an anomaly in the city grid. In the 1970s, when the Seward West PAC created a historic preservation–based redevelopment plan of the street and surrounding four blocks, Milwaukee Avenue continued its status as an anomaly.

William Ragan can be called an accidental futurist for devising what became an intimate, architecturally charming and ecological urban environment. Milwaukee Avenue today should no longer remain an anomaly but a pattern for future small-scale places existing within the large-scale urban grid. But what type of futurist was Ragan? No records have been found that describe how he thought and planned his real estate development, other than that money was his driving mechanism. He probably did not fit historian Daniel Boostin's observation that "trying to plan for the future without a sense of the past is like trying to plant cut flowers." What we do know today is that Milwaukee Avenue can serve its role in preserving Ragan's futurist legacy.

Notes

1. Lienhard, *Engines of Our Ingenuity*, 88.
2. Borchert, *Legacy of Minneapolis*, 150.
3. Alofsin, *When Buildings Speak*, 9.
4. Hamlin, *Architecture through the Ages*, 19.
5. Christensen, interview.
6. Rybczynski, *Makeshift Metropolis*.
7. Borchert, *Legacy of Minneapolis*, 150.
8. Leinberger, *Option of Urbanism*, 26.
9. Ibid., 209.
10. *This American Life*, "House Rules."
11. Leinberger, *Option of Urbnaism*, 32.
12. Ibid, 213.
13. Jacobs, *Death and Life*, 300.
14. Chandler, *Urban Homesteading*, 23.
15. Goodman, *After the Planners*, 67.
16. Ibid., 82.
17. "Compilation of the Housing and Community Development Act of 1974," 616.
18. Rybczynski, *Makeshift Metropolis*, 80.
19. Ibid., 161.
20. Brustad, interview.
21. Ibid.
22. Mack, interview.

23. Barton, interview.
24. PAC files.
25. Ibid.
26. Cox, *Storefront Revolution*, 4.
27. Rybczynski, *Makeshift Metropolis*, 89.
28. Ibid., 90.
29. Anders, interview.
30. Nathanson, "Citizens Determining Neighborhood."
31. Robbins, interview.
32. Barton, interview.
33. Robbins, interview.
34. Ibid.
35. Anders, interview.
36. Warner, interview.
37. Ibid.
38. Flint, *Wrestling with Moses*, 104.
39. PAC files.
40. Minneapolis Planning Commission, meeting minutes.
41. PAC files.
42. Ibid.
43. Minneapolis HRA, correspondence and commissioner meeting minutes.
44. Mack, interview.
45. Fournier, interview.
46. Brustad, interview.
47. Leinberger, *Option of Urbanism*, xii.
48. Chapin, *Pocket Neighborhoods*, 9.
49. Glaeser, *Triumph of the City*, 34.

Bibliography

BOOKS AND PERIODICALS

Alexander, Christopher. *Pattern Language*. New York: Oxford University Press, 1977.

Alofsin, Anthony. *When Buildings Speak*. Chicago: University of Chicago Press, 2006.

Bacon, Edmund. *Design of Cities*. New York: Viking Press, 1967.

Borchert, John R. *Legacy of Minneapolis: Preservation amid Change*. Minneapolis, MN: Voyageur Press, 1983.

Chandler, Mittie Olion. *Urban Homesteading, Programs and Politics*. New York: Greenwood Press, 1988.

Chapin, Ross. *Pocket Neighborhoods*. Newtown, CT: Taunton Press, 2011.

Collins, Cyn. *West Bank Boogie*. Minneapolis, MN: Triangle Park Creative, 2006.

Cox, Craig. *Storefront Revolution: Food Co-ops and the Counterculture*. New Brunswick, NJ: Rutgers University Press, 1994.

Flint, Anthony. *Wrestling with Moses*. New York: Random House Press, 2011.

Gibson, Andrew. Paper on Milwaukee Avenue. University of Minnesota School of Architecture, 2010.

Glaeser, Edward. *Triumph of the City*. New York: Penguin Press, 2011.

Goodman, Robert. *After the Planners*. New York: Simon & Shuster, 1971.

Hamlin, Talbot. *Architecture through the Ages*. New York: G.P. Putnam & Sons, 1953.

Harris, Marlys. "Doughnut Development in Big Urban Areas Is Waning." MinnPost, May 14, 2012.

Hess, Jeffery, and Paul Clifford Larson. *Saint Paul's Architecture*. Minneapolis: University of Minnesota Press, 2006.

Jackson, Kenneth T. *Crabgrass Frontier*. New York: Oxford University Press, 1987.

Jacobs, Jane. *The Death and Life of Great American Cities*. New York: Vintage Books, 1992.

Kunstler, James Howard. *The Geography of Nowhere*. New York: Touchstone Books, 1994.

Leinberger, Christopher. *The Option of Urbanism: Investing in a New American Dream*. Washington, D.C.: Island Press, 2009.

Lienhard, John. *Engines of Our Ingenuity*. New York: Oxford University Press, 2000.

Nathanson, Iric. "Citizens Determining Neighborhood: The Redevelopment of Seward." *Hennepin History* (Spring 1998).

Reilly, Jeri. "Temporary Home: The Immigrant in Minneapolis, 1895–1910: Milwaukee Avenue: A Case Study." 1974.

BIBLIOGRAPHY

Rybczynski, Witold. *Makeshift Metropolis*. New York: Simon & Shuster, 1994.

Stoecker, Randy. *Defending Community*. Philadelphia: Temple University Press, 1994.

OTHER RESOURCES

"Compilation of the Housing and Community Development Act of 1974." Washington, D.C.: U.S. Government Printing Office, 1974.

Minneapolis Heritage Preservation Commission. Public-hearing minutes.

Minneapolis HRA (now Community Planning and Economic Development). Correspondence and commissioner meeting minutes.

———. "Seward West Renewal Plan: Summary." September 21, 1972.

Minneapolis Planning Commission. Meeting minutes.

Seward West PAC. Meeting minutes and various file materials.

———. "Specifications for Five Milwaukee Avenue Four-Block-Area Houses." September 21, 1972.

This American Life. "House Rules." November 23, 2013.

INTERVIEWS

Rudi Anders, Seward West PAC staff member, 2010.

Don Barton, Seward West PAC staff member, 2010, 2011.

Dick Brustad, former executive director of the Minneapolis HRA's South Office, 2010.

Jack Cann, senior staff attorney, Housing Preservation Project, 2009.

Anders Christensen, 2012.

Erin Coryell, program officer, Margaret A. Cargill Foundation, 2009.

Greg Donofrio, assistant professor and director of Heritage Conservation and Preservation, University of Minnesota, 2009.

Patricia Mack, former HUD staff member, 2011.

Jeri Reilly, former Seward West PAC staff member.

Kent Robbins, Seward West PAC staff member, 2010.

Tony Scallon, Seward West PAC staff member, 2009.

Bob Scroggins, former director of Minneapolis HRA's South Office, 2009.

Perry Thorvig, former planner, Minneapolis Planning Department, 2009.

Charlie Warner, former HUD staff member, 2009.

John Wicks, Seward West PAC architecture student, 2009.

Kathy Johnson Williams, Seward West PAC staff member, 2009.

Index

About the Author

R obert Roscoe and his family moved into the Seward West neighborhood before the renewal program began, and he became a major figure in PAC's activism and in the architectural planning for the neighborhood, including the Milwaukee Avenue Four-Block Area. Robert now maintains a solo practice, Design for Preservation, in residential design and continues his involvement in local historic preservation activities.

www.ingramcontent.com/pod-product-compliance
Lightning Source LLC
Chambersburg PA
CBHW060757100426
42813CB00004B/853